# THE THEOLOGY OF ACTS
## IN ITS HISTORICAL SETTING

# THE
# THEOLOGY OF ACTS
## IN ITS HISTORICAL SETTING

J. C. O'NEILL

*2nd ed. 1970 also in stock*

LONDON
S·P·C·K
1961

First published in 1961
by S.P.C.K.
Holy Trinity Church
Marylebone Road
London N.W.1

Made and printed in Great Britain by
William Clowes and Sons, Limited, London and Beccles

*To my Wife*

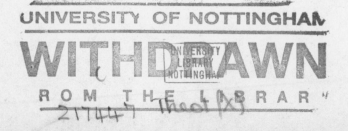

# PREFACE

I SHOULD LIKE to acknowledge the help I have received from teachers and friends in Melbourne, Göttingen, and Cambridge: from the Reverend A. L. Burns of the Australian National University, who first set me to work on the Book of Acts; the Reverend Professor J. D. McCaughey, Professor of Biblical Studies and Master of Ormond College; the Reverend J. M. Owen, Minister of Lorne, Victoria; the Reverend H. R. Wardlaw; Professor D. Dr Joachim Jeremias of Göttingen; Professor D. Ernst Käsemann, now of Tübingen; the Reverend J. N. Sanders of Peterhouse; the Reverend Professor C. F. D. Moule of Clare College; the Right Reverend Dr J. A. T. Robinson, Bishop of Woolwich; the Reverend Dr J. Y. Campbell, Professor Emeritus of Westminster College, Cambridge; and the Reverend Professor G. D. Kilpatrick of Oxford, who suggested the theme of Chapter Six. I am very grateful to all these scholars for their criticism and encouragement; none of them, of course, can be held responsible for the positions I have adopted.

*Ormond College,*                                J. C. O'N.
*Melbourne.*

v

# CONTENTS

# ABBREVIATIONS

| | |
|---|---|
| *Beginnings* | *The Beginnings of Christianity,* ed. F. J. Foakes Jackson and Kirsopp Lake |
| *E.T.* | *The Expository Times* |
| *Hdb.z.N.T.* | *Handbuch zum Neuen Testament,* ed. Hans Lietzmann, Günther Bornkamm |
| *H.T.R.* | *The Harvard Theological Review* |
| *J.B.L.* | *Journal of Biblical Literature* |
| *J.T.S.* | *The Journal of Theological Studies* |
| *N.T.S.* | *New Testament Studies* |
| *R.B.* | *Revue Biblique* |
| *Th.Wb.z.N.T.* | *Theologisches Wörterbuch zum Neuen Testament,* ed. Gerhard Kittel, G. Friedrich |
| *T.U.* | *Texte und Untersuchungen,* ed. O. von Gebhardt and A. von Harnack, etc. |
| *Z.K.G.* | *Zeitschrift für Kirchengeschichte* |
| *Z.N.W.* | *Zeitschrift für die neutestamentliche Wissenschaft* |
| *Z.Th.K.* | *Zeitschrift für Theologie und Kirche* |

# CHAPTER ONE

# THE DATE OF ACTS

THE THEOLOGY of Acts is the primary concern of this book, but I want to begin by discussing the date of Acts because the assumptions we have about date and authorship affect the way we think about the theology. Not only that; as soon as these introductory matters are raised theological issues also begin to appear, and we shall soon discover that the only way now left to solve the problem about the date of Acts is to decide where its theological affinities lie.

Neither the theology of Acts nor the date of Acts can be considered apart from the theology and date of Luke's Gospel; "Luke-Acts", to use Cadbury's term, is one work in two volumes. Luke's Gospel has traditionally been held to provide evidence of a *terminus a quo* in its reference to the fall of Jerusalem in A.D. 70. The reference is in Luke 21.20–4, and this was supposed to be a revision of Mark 13.14–20. Immediately theological questions are at stake in the technical discussion about dates; if Luke (as we shall call the author of Luke-Acts without prejudicing the question of his identity) rewrote Mark to make Mark's words refer specifically to an event which had occurred since Jesus spoke, he is without doubt a constructive theologian providing an interpretation of the significance of the prophecies; if, however, he simply chose to employ an alternative source, the question of whether or not he was a theologian remains open, as we have no certain way of telling why he preferred one account to the other.

C. H. Dodd, in an influential article, has restated the arguments of Vincent Taylor and T. W. Manson that Luke did not base his version of the Apocalypse on Mark, and that there is no need to see in Luke any reference to the fall of Jerusalem.[1] He says that both passages, Luke 21.20–4 and Mark 13.14–20, "represent diverse forms which an oracle upon the fate of Jerusalem and the Temple assumed in the pre-canonical tradition, though in the Gospel as it stands the Lucan oracle has been supplemented out of Mark".[2] The heart of Dodd's argument is an attempt to demonstrate that Luke 21.20–4 is independent of Mark. First, he states that verses 21a and 23a were inserted later into the previously existing pattern of Luke's source. He argues that they both break up the sequence of rhythmical couplets; that 21a in Luke's final form is an inadmissible hanging τότε clause in asyndeton; that the αὐτῆς and αὐτήν of 21b must now refer to Judea but can only, according to the sense, refer to Jerusalem.[3] None of these points can be sustained. Verse 21 as it stands may not be a couplet, but it makes a perfectly admissible triplet, and verse 23a is irregular in the same way as verse 24a; in any case the alleged poetic structure of the passage, with or without these two sections, is not strongly marked and cannot be used as the basis of an argument. τότε clauses can stand by themselves quite naturally (cf. Luke 11.26; 21.27). There is no reason why αὐτῆς and αὐτήν should refer to the nearest noun; grammar allows what the sense demands. Second, Dodd argues that the verbal resemblances between verse 20 and Mark 13.14 are too slight to suggest that Mark was the source,[4] and that Luke was too well schooled in his LXX to see in the phrase from Daniel and 1 Maccabees, βδέλυγμα ἐρημώσεως, any reference to the idea of Jerusalem encircled by armies.[5] Against this, it would be surprising if these verbal parallels in the middle of a chapter which usually follows the order and often follows the wording of Mark should be entirely independent. If the chief

---

[1] C. H. Dodd, "The Fall of Jerusalem and the 'Abomination of Desolation'", *The Journal of Roman Studies*, xxxvii (1947), 47–54; Vincent Taylor, *Behind the Third Gospel* (Oxford, 1926), 109–25; T. W. Manson, *The Sayings of Jesus* (London, 1949) (originally part of *The Mission and Message of Jesus*, 1937), 328–31.

[2] Dodd, op. cit., 49.     [3] Ibid., 48.     [4] Ibid., 48.

[5] Ibid., 53n.

differences could be explained by supposing that an editor knew that the predictions in Mark had not come to pass, that would be a stronger hypothesis than the complicated set of assumptions Dodd is forced to introduce: that two disconnected phrases from Mark were later inserted, so disturbing both rhythm and grammar, and that Luke suddenly abandoned Mark in favour of another source. All the differences between Luke and Mark in fact follow from Luke's historical standpoint after the fall of Jerusalem. He knew that the attempt to erect Gaius's image in the Temple had failed; he knew that the most important catastrophe in Jewish history had been the fall of Jerusalem in A.D. 70; and he knew that the catastrophe had not been the eschatological climax. It is in perfect accordance with the need to strip the fall of Jerusalem of any strict eschatological meaning that he omits Mark 13.15f and puts it in a context where it can teach that the End will be sudden and unpredictable (Luke 17.31).

The same purpose informs his rewriting of Mark 13.18–20. Dodd makes much of the fact that the references to the siege are vague and derived from the LXX, but this again accords with the assumption that an editor is at work who would avoid making predictions after the event too precise, and who regarded LXX language as the proper medium for prophecy. The very smoothness of the Lucan passage and the subtle allusions to the LXX, which Dodd adduces as reasons for believing that Luke is more primitive than the rough and disjointed Mark, are indications that Luke is later and derivative. Finally, even if Luke did possess the source which Dodd postulates, one must explain why he chose it in preference to Mark at this point; the most likely reason would seem to be that it referred better to the fall of Jerusalem.[1]

If Dodd's argument fails, we are left not only with the certainty that Luke-Acts was written after A.D. 70 but also with the certainty that the author of Luke-Acts had reflected deeply

---

[1] The Proto-Luke hypothesis, which holds that Luke had written one draft of his Gospel before he discovered Mark, is no longer tenable. Luke's Gospel was almost certainly based on Mark from the start. See G. D. Kilpatrick, *J.T.S.*, xliii (1942), esp. 36; S. MacLean Gilmour, "A Critical Re-examination of Proto-Luke", *J.B.L.*, lxvii (1948), 143–52.

on the significance of the events of history since Jesus' death and resurrection, and on the significance of Jesus' eschatological teaching in the life of the Church.[1]

There is strictly no reason why that man should not have been Luke, the companion of Paul, "the beloved physician" (Col. 4.14; 2 Tim. 4.11; Philem. 24), but doubts do begin to arise. Paul's companion, we should expect, would primarily be concerned to transmit to a later generation the excitement of the earlier age when the Apostles were alive and when, perhaps, the hope of the end was still the hope of an imminent end. The Luke of Luke-Acts is, however, a reflective theologian who seems bent on equipping the Church to live in history.

It remains possible simply to accept the second-century tradition that the author of Acts was Luke, Paul's companion, but the doubts that have already been raised, together with Cadbury's reasons for believing that the Church tradition was no more than intelligent speculation based on the internal evidence of Acts alone,[2] lead us to turn to other arguments.

Two ways of dating Acts have been often discussed, but neither has been found universally convincing. The first seeks to show that Luke was dependent on the writings of Josephus, and the main difficulty about the argument is that it turns on the proposition that Luke has misread his source.[3] The second argument is that Acts so misrepresents Paul that it must have been written when accurate knowledge of Paul's life and work had been forgotten.

This is a far more persuasive line of approach, which has been recently restated in a careful way by Ernst Haenchen.[4] The difficulty is that it depends on demonstrating a negative proposition, that the author of Acts could not have been Paul's

---

[1] Hans Conzelmann, *Die Mitte der Zeit, Studien zur Theologie des Lukas* (Tübingen, 1954), Eng. tr., *The Theology of St Luke* (London, 1960); *J.T.S.*, N.S., x (1959), 6–9.

[2] *Beginnings*, ii.250–64.

[3] *Beginnings*, ii.355–8; F. F. Bruce, New London Commentary on Acts (London, 1954), 125 and n 47.

[4] *Die Apostelgeschichte*, Kritisch-exegetischer Kommentar über das N.T. (10th ed., Göttingen, 1956), 102–6; (12th ed., 1959), 99–103. References throughout are to Haenchen's first edition, the tenth in the series.

companion, and this negative proposition is in danger of attack from two sides; it can be argued either that Luke did not understand the depths of his master's teaching, or else that he imposed on the account of Paul's activity his own theological interpretation, which was not always compatible with Paul's own views, differing at least in emphasis. Even if this negative proposition can be sustained, as I believe it can, we are not left with much guidance for the dating of Acts; all that can be asserted is that Acts was written some time after Paul's death, which in any case is rarely doubted.

The attempt will be made in this chapter to date Acts by discovering positive theological parallels between Luke-Acts and other early Christian writers. It depends on the assumption that, if it can be shown that two writers shared a whole range of presuppositions and were concerned about many of the same questions, then we may conclude that they belonged to the same generation, provided that one did not employ the other's writings. If this assumption is accepted, the discovery of close kinship between Luke-Acts and some other theologian's work, without literary dependence, will enable us to suggest the period in which Acts was composed.

It has, however, proved surprisingly difficult to discover any parallels to Acts. C. P. M. Jones[1] has drawn attention to the similarities between Luke-Acts and Hebrews in language, Christology, Eschatology, and a number of smaller points, and later we shall see some contacts between Acts and the Epistle of Barnabas, but neither of these books reflects Luke's chief interests. Neither attempts to tell the story of the early days in the life of the Church. "No contemporary and no writer before or after the writer of the canonical Acts had undertaken, as far as we know, to relate both the history of the first Christian Church and the decisive expansion of the Christian faith westwards in one consecutive narrative" (Dibelius).[2] Furthermore,

[1] "The Epistle to the Hebrews and the Lucan Writings", *Studies in the Gospels: Essays in Memory of R. H. Lightfoot* (ed. D. E. Nineham, Oxford, 1955), 113–43.

[2] *Aufsätze zur Apg.* (Göttingen, 1951), 163; cf. 11, 108f, 166; (Eng. tr., London, 1956), 192; cf. 3, 123f, 195f.

to extend Dibelius's point, no Gospel writer, apart from Luke, has considered the history of the early days of the Church of comparable importance to the history of Jesus' life, death, and resurrection. Despite the fact that in writing Acts Luke had far less material available to him and had no model to follow like Mark, he has done everything possible to give a similar structure to the Gospel and to Acts. As we shall see in more detail in Chapter Two, Acts is not simply a parallel to the Gospel, ending in Rome as the Gospel has ended in Jerusalem; if it was merely a parallel, it would inevitably be the less important part of Luke-Acts, a shadow of the Gospel original. But Acts is important in its own right as the logical completion of Jesus' journey to Jerusalem. The full significance of the central happenings at Jerusalem is not worked out in history until Paul has reached Rome. Our search for a theologian who shares Luke's presuppositions cannot end until we have found one who assumes that the missionary work of the Apostles is part of the salvation achieved by Jesus Christ in Jerusalem.

The nearest approach to Acts in the first century is in Clement of Rome's Epistle to the Corinthians. "But, to be done with the old examples, let us pass to more recent contenders; let us take the noble examples of our own generation. Because of bitter jealousy the greatest and most righteous pillars were persecuted and contended till death. Let us set before our eyes the good Apostles: Peter, who suffered not one or two but many trials because of evil jealousy and so made his witness and went to the place of glory he had earned. Because of contentious jealousy Paul demonstrated the reward for endurance: he was in bonds seven times; he was driven away; he was stoned; he was a preacher both in the East and in the West, and so he gained a nobler reputation for his faith. He taught the whole world righteousness, he came to the western goal and he made his witness before the rulers, so departing from the world and being taken up into the holy place, the greatest example of endurance" (I Clem. 5).

The point of this passage has been obscured by speculation about whether Clement is referring to the journey to Spain, which we know from Romans that Paul contemplated. If the phrase ἐπὶ τὸ τέρμα τῆς δύσεως ἐλθών does mean that Paul reached Spain, Clement is then implying that there was only one Roman visit, which occurred after the Spanish journey; like the writer of the Pastoral Epistles, he knows nothing of a release from prison in Rome, further journeys, and a new imprisonment.[1] Harrison's point that τὸ τέρμα is a very unnatural way to describe Spain (we should expect τέρματα) and that it is another of Clement's athletic metaphors, meaning the winning-post of a race, leads us to conclude that Clement is talking about Paul's arrival in Rome, and in Rome alone.[2] When he had completed his teaching mission, he came to Rome to witness to the rulers and to die a martyr's death.

Once this is established, the parallel with Acts becomes obvious. Clement is not explicit about the bitter jealousy which led to the martyrdom of Peter and Paul, but it seems that it came, in part at least, from the Jews who, more than any other group, had cause to be "jealous" of the Christians.[3] As we shall see in Chapter Three, Acts attributes all the misfortunes of the Church to Jewish opposition. Both Clement and Luke emphasize that wonderful results flowed from this "jealousy"; a witness was made and a glory attained. Both Clement and Acts put forward Peter and Paul as the leading examples, and both give Paul the pre-eminence. Clement knew that Peter was martyred in Rome, but he does not seem to have thought that the place of martyrdom was as important for Peter as it was for Paul, perhaps because Paul's martyrdom in Rome was the climax of a mission to the whole world (ὅλον τὸν κόσμον). (The reference to Peter's arrival at "the place of glory he had earned" is almost certainly not to the place where he was crucified; τόπος refers to "heaven" a few lines later (5.7), as

---

[1] Conzelmann in Dibelius, *Die Pastoralbriefe*, Hdb.z.N.T. (3rd ed., Tübingen, 1955), 3; cf. K. Holl, *Gesammelte Aufsätze zur Kirchengeschichte*, (Tübingen, 1928), 65f, n 2.

[2] P. N. Harrison, *The Problem of the Pastoral Epistles* (Oxford, 1921), 107f.

[3] Cf. J. A. Fischer, *Die Apostolischen Väter* (Darmstadt, 1956), 33 n 49.

also in John 14.2, cf. Acts 1.25.)[1] Luke simply ignores Peter's
fate, though he must have been aware of the circumstances of
his martyrdom, and he puts all the emphasis on Paul's arrival
in Rome. He would agree with Clement that Paul's universal
preaching (cf. Acts 19.10; 28.28), his arrival at Rome to be
martyred, and his witness to the rulers (cf. Acts 9.15 and *passim*)
were the most important features of his life. As Clement never
quotes or alludes to Acts in his Epistle,[2] these affinities may be
important for dating Acts.

The Pastoral Epistles stand in much the same relationship to
Luke-Acts. They share with Luke-Acts something of the same
atmosphere (for instance, in the use of eschatology to inculcate
a morality of steadfastness and temperance, and in emphasizing the importance of being in good standing with rulers).
More important, they also assume the same estimation of the
significance of Paul's work. Paul is again pictured as the model
of perseverance and endurance (2 Tim. 3.10–12), and his
arrival at Rome to defend himself before the Roman authorities marks, in some sense, the completion of the preaching to
Gentiles. In the passage in question, 2 Tim. 4.16–18, Paul is
pictured writing to Timothy from Rome during a break in the
proceedings against him.[3] "When I was making my first

---

[1] Cf. the emphasis on Rome as the place of Paul's death in Eus., *H.E.*,
ii.25.5; see H. Chadwick, "St Peter and St Paul in Rome etc.", *J.T.S.*,
N.S., viii (1957), 31–52 at 44 n 3 for the opposite view.

[2] Haenchen, op. cit., 1f; *The N.T. in the Apostolic Fathers* (Oxford, 1905),
48–50.

[3] The traditional assumption has been, on the basis of 2 Tim. 1.17, that
these words were written from Rome. There are difficulties in the way, such
as the length of time that has elapsed before the books and cloak are claimed
from Troy (4.13) and before Timothy is told of poor Trophimus's illness
(4.20), but discrepancies of this sort seem easier to explain in a pseudonymous writing than the blatant contradiction between the assumption of a
Caesarean provenance for 4.9–21 and the explicit mention of Rome in 1.17.
The final clause in 4.17 looks forward not to a Spanish journey but to the
completion of Paul's defence before the judges and his martyrdom (cf.
4.6–8); he has been delivered from the lion's mouth in the same sense as
Christ Jesus was (Psalm 22 and 2 Tim. 2.11), and his salvation through
death is certain. If it is still maintained that the author of the Pastorals
meant us to understand that these words were written from Caesarea, the

defence, no one stood by me. They all left me. (May it not be laid to their charge.) But the Lord came to my aid and strengthened me so that the preaching might be brought to its completion through me and all the Gentiles hear, and I was delivered from the lion's mouth. The Lord will deliver me from every evil thing and will bring me safely into his heavenly kingdom; to whom be glory for ever. Amen."

Contrary to the usual view, it is unlikely that the writer of the Pastoral Epistles knew and used Luke-Acts.[1] If that is so, the Pastoral Epistles may, like 1 Clement, reasonably be supposed to belong to the same period in the Church's life as Acts. But in this case we have an almost certain indication that the Pastorals were written after Luke-Acts: the Pastorals are dependent on a thorough and continuous use of the Pauline collection of letters,[2] and Luke seems to have known none of them.[3] All that we may deduce concerning the date of Acts from the theological affinity between the two sets of books is that Luke-Acts can hardly have been written long before the Pauline collection was published (if that is the right way to describe what happened), since it has in common with the Pastorals, which were written after that publication, both a general theological point of view and an estimation of the significance of Paul's work.

Clement, Luke, and the author of the Pastorals agree in

---

completion of the preaching, that all the Gentiles might hear, is still Rome, the city where Paul is to be martyred. See Conzelmann, op. cit., 94–6, where the case for Caesarea is argued; Harrison's theory that this is a genuine fragment is convincingly met by Conzelmann, 4.

[1] The quotation of the saying, "The labourer deserves his wages" in 1 Tim. 5.18 may be taken from Luke 10.7, but it is strange that the one saying of Jesus to be quoted in the Pastorals, and to be quoted as Scripture, should look so much like a common saying put into the Lord's mouth in Luke; see Conzelmann, op. cit., 62. Again, if 2 Tim. 3.11 is a summary of Acts 13.50; 14.5,19, it is strange that the writer of the Pastorals refers only to the parts of Acts where Paul is in Timothy's native area and not to those parts where Timothy was Paul's companion, Acts 16 and 17; Conzelmann, ibid., 89. 2 Tim. 4.20 seems to contradict the information about Trophimus we gather from Acts 20 and 21, especially 21.29.

[2] P. N. Harrison, op. cit., 167–75.

[3] See below, 21.

2

assuming a certain significance in the history of salvation for Paul's martyrdom in Rome. But neither Clement nor the "Pastor" did what Luke has done, and made the story of Paul an integral part of the central event, the life and death and resurrection of Jesus Christ. For that reason the assumption they share must be judged an important but minor part of Luke's theology. As we shall see in Chapter Two, the fact that Paul's martyrdom is never actually described in Acts indicates that he wished to subordinate the human example of Paul to the central event of salvation which occurred in Jerusalem. In this way he made the second part of his work an integral part of the first, rather than an appendix. The early history of the Church was put beside the Gospel history on equal terms, and so the whole journey from Galilee to Jerusalem and from Jerusalem to Rome was seen as the determinative period in the history of salvation. Clement and the "Pastor's" estimation of Paul's work seems to be accepted by Luke, but he has given it a further significance in the history of salvation which we do not find in them.

The first writer, apart from Luke, to assume that the world mission of the Apostles should be told in the same breath as the history of Jesus' death, resurrection, and ascension is Justin Martyr.[1] In the Apology he writes, "After his crucifixion even all his friends deserted, and denied him. But later, when he rose from the dead and appeared to them, he taught them to read the prophecies in which all these things that had happened were foretold. They saw him return to heaven and believed and, when they had received power which he sent from heaven to them, they went to every nation of men and taught these things, and were called 'Apostles'" (50.12; cf. Dial. 53.5). The missionary activity of the Apostles "from Jerusalem" is as much part of the history of salvation as the work of Jesus. The mission of the Apostles was also foretold in the O.T. To prove

[1] In Matthew the world mission is commanded, not related. Marcion's name should also be mentioned here. By publishing his "Gospel" and "Apostle", he linked together the work of Jesus with the work of his Apostle in the same way as Luke and Justin; cf. John Knox, *Marcion and the N.T.* (Chicago, 1942), chap. v.

this Justin quotes Isa. 65.2 and writes, "And there is evidence to convince you (Trypho) that this has come to pass: for men, twelve in number, went out from Jerusalem into the world; they were uneducated (ἰδιῶται) and not good speakers, but by God's power they made known to every nation of men how they had been sent by the Messiah to teach the entire Word of God . . ." (Apol. 39.2f; cf. 42.4; 45.5; 49.5; 50.12; 53.3; 61.9; 67.3; Dial. 109.1; 110.2).

There are many more parallels, but enough have been given to show that the writer of Acts and Justin share an important theological point of view. Without this theological understanding of the connection between the work of Christ and the work of the Apostles, Luke-Acts would be inconceivable.

This concurrence at a crucial point is backed by a number of other theological and factual agreements. The first passage quoted from Justin, Apol. 50.12, provides evidence of a detailed theology of Jesus' resurrection which in the N.T. is peculiar to Luke-Acts. With it should be compared Dialogue 53.5; 106.1; the chief Lucan passages to compare are Luke 24.25–7 and 44–6. The agreements may be summarized in six points. First, Luke and Justin state that the chief business of the risen Messiah was to persuade the Apostles that his suffering was foretold; in Justin this persuasion is all the more necessary because, after the crucifixion, they had not only deserted but had all denied him.[1] Second, they both greatly elaborate and illustrate the primitive statement that all that had happened was "according to the Scriptures", and the discovery of relevant passages plays a central part in the theology of both writers (cf. also Heb. and 2 Pet.). Third, they both state that during the resurrection discussion Jesus referred back to his own predictions of suffering (Dial. 53.5; 106.1; a minor point, and partially paralleled in the angel's words, Mark 16.7). Fourth, both explicitly record Jesus' ascension (see also Dial.

[1] A. Ritschl, *Das Evangelium Marcions und das kanonische Evangelium des Lukas* (Tübingen, 1846), 150, notes that this is foreign to the canonical gospels. Perhaps it is simply an extension of Mark 14.27,50 and Peter's denial; there may be traces of post-crucifixion denial in the road to Emmaus story.

108.2). Fifth, both state that after the ascension the Apostles received power from above. Sixth, in both it is said that the Apostles went into all the world to teach what Jesus had persuaded them was true; in both Luke and Justin this is principally the fulfilment of O.T. prophecy in the events of Jesus' passion. None of these points, taken singly, is exactly paralleled elsewhere in the N.T.; that not only the individual points but also the same combination should be found in Justin is a most remarkable coincidence. The coincidence is even more significant for our purpose because this theology of the work of Christ is found at the centre of Luke-Acts and is presupposed throughout, particularly in the speeches in Acts.

A further significant similarity between the two writers is found in their attitude to Jews and Gentiles. In Acts, as in Luke's Gospel,[1] it is assumed that the Jews have rejected the gospel and that the Gentiles will receive it—or at least Luke believes that the Gentiles can be persuaded to receive the gospel, and he insists that they show no ineradicable opposition to it. That the same position is fundamental in Justin is shown by the fact that he writes an Apology for the Romans but a Dialogue with a Jew.[2] "The Jews", he says, "had the prophecies and were ever expecting the Messiah to be at hand; they not only failed to recognize him but also ill-treated him. But the Gentiles, who had never heard anything about the Messiah until the Apostles came from Jerusalem and told them about him and imparted the prophecies, were filled with joy and faith and said farewell to idols and dedicated themselves to the unbegotten God through the Messiah" (Apol. 49.5). We could

[1] See, for example, the first Amen saying in Luke (Luke 4.24); "The Six Amen Sayings in Luke", *J.T.S.*, N.S., x (1959), 2–4.

[2] F. Overbeck, "Ueber das Verhältniss Justins des Martyrers zur Apg.", *Zeitschrift für wissenschaftliche Theologie*, xv (Leipzig, 1872), 305–49 at 342: "So in point of fact it seems that, to Justin, the enmity of the Gentiles and their government to Christians was something which was scarcely explicable, which was only grudgingly recognized, and which one hoped still to change (which is, of course, the aim of the Apologies). On the other hand the antagonism shown by the Jews against Christians is, as it were, a natural growth; one cannot expect it to be overcome before the end of the present world-order with Christ's return."

hardly find a clearer statement of one of the leading themes in Acts: how the Church discovered its proper place in the Gentile world.

We should conclude by noting six coincidences in detail between Justin's works and Acts. First, Justin argues from a Psalm of David to Jesus in the same way as Peter argues at Pentecost (Acts 2.25–32): "And again in other words, through another prophet, he (the Spirit) says, 'They pierced my hands and feet, and cast lots for my clothing.' Now David, the King and Prophet, who said these things, suffered none of them; but Jesus Christ stretched out his hands and was crucified by the Jews who reviled him and denied that he was the Messiah" (Apol. 35.5,6).[1] Second, both note that the Apostles were uneducated (ἰδιῶται: Acts 4.13; Apol. 39.3). Third, both employ the common idea, probably going back to Socrates, "It is necessary to obey God rather than men" (Acts 5.29; 4.19; Dial. 80.3; 1 Clem. 14.1; 2 Clem. 4.4).[2] Fourth, in Justin and Acts (and in Ignatius) we find it explicitly stated that Jesus both "ate and drank" with his disciples after his resurrection (Acts 10.41; Dial. 51.2; Smyrn. 3.3).

Fifth, Justin provides a clue to the riddle of "the Unknown God" in Acts 17.23. It is doubtful whether there was an actual inscription in Athens in the singular but, whatever the historical facts, the widespread literary tradition was that there was an altar in Athens dedicated to "the Unknown Gods".[3] Luke's apologetic purpose would be thwarted if his educated non-Christian readers should at any point in the speech have cause to suspect that Paul was arguing from an assumption which the Athenians did not accept. If the speech was to retain its effectiveness, Luke must have been able to count on his audience accepting the premise that the Athenians (and

---

[1] Ibid., 347.

[2] Beginnings, iv.45.

[3] K. Lake, Beginnings, v.240–6; and B. Gärtner, The Aeropagus Speech and Natural Revelation (Uppsala, 1955) set out the evidence. It is unlikely that the words of Diogenes Laertius refer to any particular altar inscription; the patristic evidence gives strong support to the general tradition that the Athenians had altars dedicated to "the Unknown Gods".

therefore all men of a philosophical temper) had at least enter-
tained belief in an "Unknown God". Justin Martyr supplies
evidence that Christian apologists were able to appeal to such
a belief, although his argument is based on the writings of
Plato rather than on an inscription. After pointing out that
Socrates was accused of the same crime as Christians, that of
introducing new divinities, he writes, "But he taught men to
escape from wicked demons and those who did what the poets
related, and he drove out of the state Homer and the other
poets. Instead, he exhorted them to seek full knowledge, by
the exercise of reason, of God who was unknown to them (πρὸς
θεοῦ δὲ τοῦ ἀγνώστου αὐτοῖς διὰ λόγου ζητήσεως ἐπίγνωσιν
προὐτρέπετο), saying, 'It is not easy to find the Father and
Maker of all nor when he is found is it safe to tell everyone'"
(Appendix to the Apology, the so-called Second Apology,
10.6). There is no sign that Justin is here dependent on Acts.
One may suspect, without being able to demonstrate it, that
Luke used this sort of apologetic argument as one of his starting
points in constructing the speech at Athens; he has dramatized
the argument by supposing, on the basis of the current story
that the Athenians had sacrificed to Unknown Gods, that the
traditional Platonic monotheism had found expression in an
altar "to the Unknown God". Whether or not this hypothesis
can be sustained, it remains significant that both Luke and
Justin appeal to an Athenian belief in the Unknown God.

Finally, we find in Justin's Dialogue with Trypho 39.4 a
dramatic device similar to that which Luke employs when Festus
intervenes in Paul's speech to Agrippa (Acts 26.25). Trypho
accuses Justin of being beside himself, to which Justin replies,
"Listen, my friend, I am not mad or beside myself", before
continuing his argument. This seems to be a stock apologetic
situation which, no doubt, occurred often enough, but which
may have been a common ingredient in the accounts of debates
held between Christians and unbelievers. It is possible that it
goes back to Paul, but Justin seems to be unaware of any such
association.

In none of these six cases is there any indication that Justin was dependent on Acts. He makes no reference to the context in which the statements occur in Acts, and he often uses as his own the ideas which are ascribed by Acts to Paul and the Apostles (in the first, third, fifth, and sixth examples above).

The case for literary dependence rests on an examination of Apol. 50.12, which has been quoted above. Haenchen holds that this passage proves that Justin knew Acts. "The substance of Luke 23.49a is cited in the account of the passion story; Luke 24.25,44f is clearly employed; and the ascension and gift of the Spirit are reported with verbal reminiscence of Acts 1.8, δύναμιν . . . λαβόντες corresponding to the λήμψεσθε δύναμιν of Acts."[1] Against this argument there are three objections. First, Luke 23.49a, apart from the fact that it uses γνωστοί and not γνώριμοι for Jesus' followers, does not say or imply that the disciples deserted Jesus and denied him, as Justin does. Second, the only pair of words common to Luke-Acts and Justin in this passage is δύναμιν λαβόντες. In Acts these words are spoken by Jesus, and it is incredible that Justin should reproduce as his own comment words which were attributed to the Lord in his source. Finally, it is surprising, if Justin knew Acts 2, that he neglected to say that this "power" was the power of the Holy Spirit. There is no evidence that Justin cited Acts or even knew of its existence.

In his discussion of this passage, Overbeck comes to the conclusion that, if it is a citation at all, it is a citation of Luke's Gospel and not of Acts. Despite the absence of evidence, however, he is compelled to hold that Justin knew Acts. "It is impossible to imagine", he writes, "that a man in Justin's position, who made use of Luke's Gospel, could not know something of a book which originally formed the continuation of the Gospel, or at least purported to be its continuation."[2]

There are at least three answers to Overbeck's dilemma. The first is his own. He argues that Justin knew Acts but deliberately

---

[1] Haenchen, op. cit., 7. Cadbury in his review of Haenchen, *J.B.L.*, lxxvi (1957), 65, doubts Haenchen's case; see also *The Book of Acts in History* (London, 1955), 157.

[2] Op. cit., 316.

rejected it because he had succumbed to Jewish propaganda against Paul and because he was engaged in answering Marcion. Only in this way can he reconcile the fact of the enormous area of agreement between the two writers, in their attitude to heathen culture, to the Jews, and to the Romans, with the determined avoidance of Acts by Justin.[1] The weakness of Overbeck's case is that nowhere does Justin explicitly argue against those Christians who presumably espoused the book. He was not afraid of mentioning differing groups and sects within the Church, but he completely ignores Acts and those who read and treasured it.

The second way out is to suppose that Acts acquired canonical status much later than Luke's Gospel, and was ignored until its association with the third Gospel ensured it a place in the canonical collection.[2] The question at once arises, however, of why Acts should be ignored and the Gospel recognized. There seems to be no reason why Acts should have been judged useless for preaching and teaching; if it had no special authority, it was at least edifying, interesting, and relevant to the life of the Church. If Justin knew of it at all, his own special interests would surely have led him to quote from it or draw on it in some other way. Despite the weaknesses of the second argument, however, we should probably have to accept it if no other possibility could be found.

The third way out of Overbeck's dilemma is to deny his major premise, that Justin knew Luke's Gospel. The fact that Justin makes no use of Acts then becomes perfectly explicable; as he did not know Luke's Gospel, there is no need to be puzzled by the evidence that he did not use Acts. The Appendix is devoted to the detailed discussion necessary to prove this point. The fact that he makes no *use* of Luke, which is all that is proved in the Appendix, indicates that he had never *known* Luke; as he at times harmonizes two sources, Matthew and his other Gospel, he would probably not have objected to harmonizing a third, if it was available. Should it be maintained that

---

[1] Ibid., 343 and *passim.*
[2] Haenchen, op. cit., 7, following Dibelius.

Justin *knew* both Luke and Acts but deliberately ignored them, the case we are about to put forward would stand: the similarities between Luke-Acts and Justin's writings could still not be explained on the basis of direct literary influence, but only on the basis of a common background of ideas. It remains much more probable that Justin failed to use Luke and Acts because he had never read them.

Given these two propositions (1) that there is a close similarity in the basic theology of Luke and Justin, as well as in minor matters like the sort of apologetic arguments they use and (2) that neither has read the writings of the other, we have good reason to conclude that they belong to the same generation. Harnack's dating of Justin's Apology and Dialogue is generally accepted. The Apology (which is one work with an appendix, not two) he puts "a few years after 150", and the Dialogue between 150 and 160; he believes that Justin became a Christian about A.D. 133.[1] I think that these dates are rather late, and that the Apology might well have been written either in the first year of Antonius Pius's reign (July 138–July 139) as the omission of "Caesar" in Marcus's title in the dedication seems to indicate, or in the first three or four years of the same reign (not later than July 142) as Eusebius maintained in his *Chronicon*,[2] but, whatever the conclusion, Justin's "generation", the generation which formed and shared his Christian

---

[1] *Geschichte der Altchristlichen Literatur bis Eusebius*, Part ii, *Die Chronologie* (2nd ed., Leipzig, 1897, repr. 1958), 274–84.

[2] Ibid., ii.29,57f. Harnack once argued from Justin's silence about Marcion's residence in Rome that Marcion had not yet arrived when the Apology was written; ibid., ii.277 and n 2. That, of course, would conflict with the dating of the Apology which he later adopted (ii.276ff) but, as his case for this dating stands and falls on the assumption that Marcus Aurelius had to be in full philosophical flight and that Lucius, the other person mentioned in the dedication, had to be rather more than eight years old before he could receive a dedication (whereas he seems to be included simply because he was son of the *philosopher*-emperor Aelius Verus as well as adopted son of Antonius Pius; ibid., ii.280), the late dating is not as obvious as has often been thought. The Appendix to the Apology (the so-called Second Apology) contains a number of indications of a later date, but it is by no means certain that it was first published at the same time as the (First) Apology.

theology, can hardly have flourished earlier than about A.D. 115 or later than about A.D. 170. Luke probably wrote Luke-Acts at some time during this period. It is very unlikely that he wrote earlier than 115; he probably wrote some time after this date, because the earlier Luke-Acts was written, the more likely it is that Justin would have heard of the work.

If we can determine the first witness to the existence of Luke's Gospel, we shall be able to put forward an upper dating, and to fix the composition of Luke-Acts within narrower limits. Some scholars have argued that Papias knew Luke's Gospel,[1] but this is an argument from silence. Papias mentions only the traditions about the composition of the Gospels according to Matthew and Mark (Eus., *H.E.*, iii.39.15f), and it is precarious to argue that he omitted Luke because he disapproved of the author's association with St Paul.

With Justin eliminated, the next possible witness to Luke's Gospel is Marcion, who traditionally is supposed to have put forward a drastically edited edition of Luke as "The Gospel". It has, however, been doubted whether Marcion did indeed employ Luke's Gospel, and John Knox has revived the theory that Marcion was using the shorter Gospel which was later expanded into our canonical Luke.[2] There seem to be three preliminary objections which can be made to this theory. First, an objection Knox himself tries to meet.[3] If Luke, and therefore Acts, was edited to meet the claims of Marcion, the fact that Acts makes no use of the Pauline epistles, which Marcion had also edited, becomes even more difficult to explain than before. At any time before Marcion it is conceivable that the Pauline collection could have been unknown to the author of Acts, but after Marcion this becomes almost impossible. I cannot believe that he deliberately ignored Paul's letters.

Second, if Luke's Gospel was finally expanded and edited after Marcion, the Marcionite Christians would be perfectly

[1] Jülicher-Fascher, *Einleitung*, (7th ed., Tübingen, 1931), 312; Westcott; Walter Bauer.

[2] *Marcion and the N.T.; An Essay in the Early History of the Canon* (Chicago, 1942), esp. chap. iv.

[3] Op. cit., 132–9.

well aware of the fact. The orthodox defence of the four Gospels as ancient and apostolic would be open to such an obvious rebuttal that it is difficult to imagine it being made in this form at all. If such a defence was possible, then the obvious Marcionite objection cannot have been possible; there is no reason to doubt the statement made from Irenaeus onwards that Marcion's Gospel was based on the Gospel of Luke.

Third, every process of editing a Gospel about which we possess evidence has involved the shortening of the source. Matthew and Luke have each omitted some incidents and sayings from Mark. Knox admits that Marcion, who on his theory was using an earlier and shorter edition of the canonical Luke, omitted some parts of this short edition. It would be very surprising, then, if Knox's later editor, in producing the canonical Luke, had not omitted something from the shorter Gospel which was his (and Marcion's) source; if he did omit any parts, they would probably be among those which Marcion retained. We should expect, on Knox's theory, that Marcion's Gospel would contain some incidents or sayings which are not found in our present edition of Luke. The fact that Marcion's Gospel (as far as it can be recovered) contains no saying or incident which is not in Luke, in one form or another, counts against Knox's thesis.

There is, however, an important fact about Marcion's Gospel which lends powerful support to the theory Knox has revived, and which the usual interpretation underestimates. A large number of Marcion's changes seem to have no doctrinal motive, and this raises difficulties for a theory which ascribed the changes to an arbitrary desire to alter Jesus' words to fit a particular theological point of view. If a number of important differences between Marcion's Gospel and our form of Luke's Gospel cannot be explained as alterations which Marcion might make in Luke to suit his own theology, it becomes much more of an open question whether Marcion had altered Luke or Luke Marcion. For the reasons given, it still seems more likely that Marcion had altered our Luke, but the investigation of Justin's Gospel sources suggests another answer to the problem. In two cases we have found that Marcion's version of Luke, while retaining traces of the Lucan framework, agrees with Justin.[1] As Justin seems here to be employing his special Gospel source (a source which was probably used by Luke), we should probably conclude that Marcion is editing Luke by means of this older source. Some of the differences between Luke's Gospel and Marcion's version may be due to Marcion's use of sources which he believed were more reliable, in order to correct Luke.

This last point is important for estimating the lowest possible interval between the composition of Luke and the issuing of Marcion's Gospel. Assuming that Marcion's Gospel was published early in the 140's, and that it was a revision of Luke's Gospel, we should be able to fix a time after which Luke could not have been written. On one view of Marcion's work, he has selected the established Gospel which suited his purpose best and arbitrarily changed it whenever he wished. But it is not necessary to hold that Marcion was trying to produce an uncorrupted version of Luke's Gospel as such; it is more likely that he intended to produce a pure version of the most authentic Gospel possible. It is not necessary, that is, to assume that Luke had attained any sort of canonical acceptance: indeed, there is no evidence that any of the Gospels were quoted with canonical authority by this date.[2] We do not know why Marcion chose Luke's Gospel as the basis of his own, but his silence about Lucan authorship is evidence against the theory that he chose it because he believed it was the work of St Paul's companion.[3] There is therefore no need to assume that Marcion's use of Luke implies that Luke has been in circulation for a long time or that it had any strong ecclesiastical authority. Luke-Acts need not have been written very long before A.D. 140. On the other hand we are required to allow at least time for it to have

---

[1] The two cases are Luke 10.22; Dial. 100.1; and Luke 18.18f; Apol. 16.7; Dial. 101.2; see the Appendix and Tables IV and X.

[2] H. Köster, *Synoptische Überlieferung bei den Apostolischen Vätern*, *T.U.*, v.10 (=65.Band) (Berlin, 1957).

[3] Cf. H. J. Cadbury, *The Book of Acts in History* (London, 1955), 145f.

become fairly well known and respected in Christian circles, time for it to have gained the sort of following which would justify Marcion in making it the basis of a new edition. It is hard to imagine this condition being fulfilled if Luke-Acts had been issued less than ten years before Marcion's edition, and we suggest very tentatively that Luke could not have been written later than A.D. 130.

The *terminus a quo* for Luke-Acts is about A.D. 115 and the *terminus ad quem* is about A.D. 130, but the naming of these dates gives an air of precision to the case which is scarcely warranted. More important than the dates are the arguments, that Luke and Justin Martyr held common theological positions without being dependent on each other, and that Luke-Acts was completed in time for Luke to be used by Marcion.

There remains one important objection to dating Luke-Acts late enough to be part of a theological movement still represented in the writings of Justin Martyr. The writer of Acts seems to know nothing of Paul's Epistles. Some critics have detected traces of influence of the Epistles, but if Luke knew anything at all of any one of them he would almost certainly have made a great deal of use of it, and have looked for others; only slight dependence means no dependence. Luke-Acts must, then, belong to an age when Paul's letters were not generally known. Largely as a result of the work of E. J. Goodspeed, it is now coming to be accepted that the Pauline letters were rescued from obscurity and "published" as a collection about A.D. 90.[1] If Goodspeed's thesis is accepted, Luke-Acts cannot be later than about A.D. 90.[2]

Without entering into a full discussion of Goodspeed's theory, some arguments against this early dating for the formation of the corpus should be mentioned. Goodspeed seems to be on firm ground when he denies Harnack's theory of the gradual

---

[1] E. J. Goodspeed, *An Introduction to the New Testament* (Chicago, 1937), etc. For a favourable British report see C. L. Mitton, *The Formation of the Pauline Corpus of Letters* (London, 1955).

[2] E.g., Haenchen, op. cit., 106.

building up of the collection of letters, but he has probably placed the date of "publication" too soon.

In attempting to show that "the letters of Paul had disappeared from Christian consciousness" at the time the synoptic Gospels were written and that they suddenly reappeared in all the Christian writings after A.D. 90, Goodspeed and his supporters are forced to rely on an argument from silence. "If failure to quote from a Pauline letter proved ignorance of it, the evidence of the Apostolic Fathers would support Lake and Harrison in the claim that partial collections existed in different centres, before the complete Corpus was formed. It does not, however, prove this. Any one of the Apostolic Fathers may have known all ten epistles without happening to reflect more than one or two."[1] This argument is true as far as it goes: the silence of an Apostolic Father about any of the letters of Paul does not necessarily prove that he did not know it. But we must go on to ask whether there is other evidence to settle the question one way or the other.

The three Apostolic Fathers who particularly concern us are Clement of Rome, Ignatius, and Polycarp. The evidence of the way they use Paul's Epistles suggests that the first two knew only some of them and that Polycarp knew all of them. First, the conclusions of the Committee of the Oxford Society of Historical Theology which investigated the question in 1905 point in this direction.[2] They have classified the degree of probability that an author should have known each book of the N.T. by using the letters A to D, class A at one end indicating that there could be "no reasonable doubt", and class D at the other that "the evidence appeared too uncertain to allow any reliance to be placed upon it".[3] The evidence for the use of Paul's ten epistles by the three authors we are considering may be set out as follows.[4]

---

[1] Mitton, op. cit., 23.
[2] *The N.T. in the Apostolic Fathers* (Oxford, 1905).
[3] Ibid., Preface.
[4] Ibid., 137.

|  | A | B | C | D |
|---|---|---|---|---|
| 1 Clement | Rom. | — | — | 2 Cor. Gal. |
|  | 1 Cor. |  |  | Eph. Phil. |
|  |  |  |  | Col. |
| Ignatius | 1 Cor. | Eph. | Rom. 2 Cor.? | Col. 1, 2 |
|  |  |  | Gal. Phil. | Thess.? |
|  |  |  |  | Philem.? |
| Polycarp | 1 Cor. | Rom. 2 Cor. | — | Col. |
|  |  | Gal. Eph. |  |  |
|  |  | Phil. 2 Thess. |  |  |

On the face of it, this table indicates that there is a high probability that 1 Clement knew Romans and 1 Corinthians and that Ignatius knew 1 Corinthians (and Ephesians?), and a considerably lower probability that they knew the rest; there is a distinct contrast between the force of the evidence that they knew one or two epistles and the evidence that they knew the others, especially in 1 Clement. For Polycarp, on the other hand, the probability is high that he knew a large number of the epistles, as most of the evidence is concentrated under categories A and B, and it shows that he used seven out of the ten.

Second, the manner in which these writers refer to the Epistles offers some indication of whether they knew the whole collection or only one or two of the letters.

Clement of Rome refers specifically to 1 Corinthians in his own letter to the Corinthians. He writes, "Take up the epistle of blessed Paul the Apostle" (1 Clem. 47.1). If Clement and the Corinthians had recently witnessed the rediscovery and publication of a collection of Paul's epistles, it seems likely that Clement would have made his reference to 1 Corinthians more explicit. He would probably have written something like, "Take up *your* epistle of Paul." The method he used to refer to 1 Corinthians implies that the Corinthians possessed only one of Paul's epistles (or one limited group of epistles, those addressed to them). Similarly, if Paul's letters had recently been published in a collection, one would expect Clement to acknowledge any extended quotation from them. Instead, Romans 1.29–32 is incorporated into 1 Clement 35.5 with no indication of its source. (The argument is weakened, but not demolished, if both writers are making independent use of a common list of vices.)

The one explicit reference to the epistles of Paul in Ignatius shows the same features. In his letter to the Ephesians, 12.2, he refers to "Paul . . . who in every epistle mentions you in Christ Jesus".[1] Paul only mentioned the Ephesians in 1 Cor. 15.32 and 16.8, and this is the one Pauline epistle which it is extremely probable that Ignatius knew.[2] Ignatius's statement is pardonable exaggeration only in the writing of a man who knew in general that Paul wrote a number of letters and that he spent some time in Ephesus, without knowing much more; the inaccuracy is extremely difficult to understand in the work of a man who had read the great new collection of Paul's letters, published in his life-time.

When we turn to the epistle of Polycarp, an entirely different picture meets us. Not only are Ephesians, Galatians, 1 Corinthians (and 1 Timothy) explicitly cited but a standard citation formula is employed: εἰδότες ὅτι (1.3; 4.1; 5.1; cf. 9.2; 11.2; 12.1). The use of such a formula implies that the recipients of Polycarp's letter could verify the references for themselves, that they possessed a collection of Paul's letters. "It appears that the collection of the Epistles of Paul was as good as closed by II Polycarp, something that it was not possible to say for Ignatius. . . . Polycarp also assumes that the recipients in Philippi know the collection and recognize it."[3]

If Polycarp is the first of the Fathers to use a published collection of Paul's letters, we are now in a position to suggest a date for the formation of the corpus. P. N. Harrison[4] has put

---

[1] See W. Bauer, *Hdb.z.N.T.*, *Ergänzungsband* (Tübingen, 1920), 212.
[2] The references to the Ephesians in 1 Tim. 1.3; 2 Tim. 1.16ff; 4.19f and in the opening of Eph. are probably not by Paul.
[3] J. A. Fischer, *Die Apostolischen Väter* (Darmstadt, 1956), 239.
[4] *Polycarp's Two Epistles to the Philippians* (Cambridge, 1936).

forward a persuasive case for regarding the first twelve chapters of Polycarp's epistle as a later composition. Chiefly on the basis of a reference to Marcion in 7.1 (cf. Eus., *H.E.*, iv.14.7; Iren. iii.3.4), he dates this second letter about A.D. 135.[1]

On the basis of this argument it is no longer necessary to suppose that Luke-Acts must have been written before A.D. 95. Since the first witness to the existence of the Pauline corpus is the second epistle of Polycarp, about A.D. 135, the author of Luke-Acts could still have written in ignorance of Paul's letters between A.D. 115 and 130, the limiting dates which were suggested earlier.

But, it might be asked, is it really possible that the author of Acts could have failed to discover and use at least one of Paul's letters if he was working not long after Clement and Ignatius had used Romans and 1 Corinthians? The Pauline corpus may not yet have been published and made widely known, but is it conceivable that Luke should have been unable to use some of the letters—if indeed he wrote as late as this?

These are difficult questions, but there is evidence that it could have been possible for such a late writer not to have had access to even one Pauline epistle. This possibility existed because there was no universal interest in the work of Paul and because a church which still treasured one of his letters would probably have felt no need to send copies of it to other churches. Proof and illustration is found in the writings of Justin Martyr.

[1] Fischer, op. cit., 234–8, accepts the two-fold division of the epistle, but argues for a date for 2 Polyc. one or two years after 1 Polyc. Peter Meinhold, Article "Polykarpos", Pauly-Wissowa, *Realencyclopädie der classischen Altertumswissenschaft*, 42. Halbband (Stuttgart, 1952), coll. 1662–93 at 1681–8, supports Harrison's argument that the second letter to the Philippians was written long after the first as an answer to Marcion. He denies Harrison's contention that Marcion's doctrine was still undeveloped, but agrees with him in placing this attack on Marcion after the famous encounter between the two men, which, he argues, occurred in Asia Minor and before Marcion reached Rome. While agreeing that "2 Phil." is an attack on Marcion, I am not sure that it is possible to date it so precisely; it may well have been written later, when Marcion's break with Rome made his threat to the Church's life far clearer and when it was necessary to show that the leaders of the orthodox church made no claim to rival "the wisdom of the blessed and glorious Paul" (Polyc., *ad Phil.*, 3.2).

3

Justin almost certainly wrote after the Pauline collection was published, and not only does he never quote Paul but he never even mentions him. Attempts have been made to explain this silence on the assumption that Justin was familiar with Paul's work and writings; Overbeck[1] argued that Justin had succumbed to the attacks of the Jewish opponents of Paul and that he did not want to prejudice his case against Marcion by quoting the Apostle, while Harnack,[2] in rejecting Overbeck's position, argued that Justin omitted to mention the honoured Apostle because he was able to find nothing of use in Paul's attitude to the Law and Judaism, and consequently, by remaining silent, could avoid bringing down on his own head the whole weight of Jewish prejudice against Paul. Harnack admitted that Justin's silence was possible because Paul's writings were not yet regarded as canonical, but the evidence seems to require a more radical conclusion than that. Both Harnack and Overbeck have advanced reasons why Justin might decide to set aside Paul, but in both arguments it is granted that Paul's position would have been relevant to Justin's case, if not for Justin himself in the first place, for his opponents, and therefore for him to answer in the long run. The only satisfactory explanation of Justin's silence is that Paul was not an influence on his theology; that Paul's writings were not in use in his Church; that Paul was not especially remembered for his missionary work; that Paul was not quoted against Justin's church by Jewish controversialists; and that Paul was not counted as one of the Apostles.[3] Of course this also involves the assumption that Marcion's edition of Paul was not the dominant issue for Justin; but it might not yet have

[1] "Ueber das Verhältnis Justins des Märtyrers zur Apg.", *Zeitschrift für wissenschaftliche Theologie*, xv (1872), 343.

[2] *Judentum und Judenchristentum in Justins Dialog mit Trypho*, *T.U.*, iii. 9 (= 39.Band) (Leipzig, 1913), 50f.

[3] This last point is not as scandalous as it sounds, because Acts does not count Paul among the Apostles—meaning the reconstituted Twelve—and calls him an apostle only in a different sense; J. Y. Campbell, article "Apostle", *A Theological Word Book of the Bible*, ed. A. Richardson (London, 1950), 20f; Haenchen, op. cit., 102f. This is one of the soundest reasons for believing that the author of Acts was not Paul's companion.

become a dominant issue for Marcion himself, since he seems not to have published his "Gospel" and "Apostle" until the decade after his excommunication in Rome (A.D. 144), and long before then to have worked out his peculiar theological position.[1] It is all the more likely if Marcion had not yet been expelled from the Roman Church when Justin wrote.

The fact that Paul's epistles are quoted in 1 Clement and Ignatius, and that Paul's work is held in high regard by Luke shows that his influence did not entirely disappear, but the absence of reference to him or his position in the first two Gospels, in John, and in the Apocalypse,[2] as well as in Justin Martyr, is proof that it was possible for Christian writers to ignore Paul or perhaps even to be in ignorance of his work and writings. Luke seems to be a mid-way case in that he knows of Paul but has not read his epistles, but the other writers who show no trace of Pauline influence may have been in the same position, as any influence they betray would be not by mentioning Paul's name but by referring to his statements and arguments: they too might have known his reputation as a missionary without having read his epistles.

The silence of Justin about Paul indicates two things: that the hero of one part of the Church could be as good as unknown in another part; and that even the collection and publication of the letters of Paul took time to affect the whole Church. If we

---

[1] Clem. Alex., *Strom.*, vii.17.106f; Tert., *de praescr.*, 30; *adv. Marc.*, i.1; iv.4; Harnack, *Geschichte der altchristlichen Literatur bis Eusebius*, ii, *Die Chronologie* (2nd ed., Leipzig, 1897, repr. 1958), 298–310. Harnack later maintained that Marcion prepared his "Gospel" and "Epistle" in Rome during the quiet years before his excommunication (139 to 144), the argument being that only in quiet could one produce such comprehensive and weighty works; *Marcion: Das Evangelium vom fremden Gott*, *T.U.*, iii.15 (=45.Band) (Leipzig, 1924), 25f. The deduction from Tertullian that the heretical works were only published after the excommunication (though they may have been prepared earlier) presumably still stands.

[2] Goodspeed (see Mitton, op. cit., 32f) believes that the seven letters at the beginning of the Apocalypse show the influence of the Pauline corpus of seven, but it is probable that the influence, if any, runs the other way; the author of the Apocalypse is interested in the symbolic significance of seven and, on the other hand, it probably required some juggling to find seven members for the Pauline corpus.

are right to assume that, although Clement of Rome and Ignatius used one or two letters of Paul, the Pauline collection was not published until some time before A.D. 135, it is possible in the light of the evidence from Justin to imagine Luke composing his two volumes without having access to any of Paul's letters. Clement and Ignatius were fortunate to have read some of Paul, but both the absence of interest in Paul in parts of the Church and the slowness with which writings treasured in one area were circulated to other areas show that it would have been quite possible for an author writing about Paul in this period to have written without knowing the epistles.

We have used a preliminary analysis of Luke's theology to help fix the date of composition of his writings. Our conclusions must be tested by further discussion of the theology, and by comparing it with the writings of those who, we now have reason to believe, were Luke's contemporaries.

## APPENDIX TO CHAPTER ONE

### Did Justin Martyr use Luke's Gospel?

After tracing briefly the history of the discussion of this question, we shall try to establish five points. First, Justin did not use the third Gospel as a source. Second, he employed a source (or sources) also used by Luke. Third, he harmonized his own source with Matthew as he wrote; he was not copying from an existing Gospel-harmony. Fourth, Justin shared with the author of Luke-Acts a number of unwritten traditions. Fifth, a subsidiary point, Marcion edited Luke's Gospel in the light of Justin's other source (or sources).

Albrecht Ritschl, in the first book he wrote, denied that Justin used Luke's Gospel.[1] His case rests mainly on the contradictions between Justin and Luke: Justin's statements that Jesus was born near, not in, Bethlehem and that he was descended from David through his mother and not through

---

[1] *Das Evangelium Marcions und das kanonische Evangelium des Lukas* (Tübingen, 1846), especially 135–51.

Joseph, and the assertion, in Dial. 103, that no one came to Jesus' aid when he was arrested, which conflicts with Luke 22.49–51.[1] He argues further that, though many of the individual expressions in Justin's citations of the sayings of Jesus tend towards Matthew, the Gospel he remembers best is Marcion's, for it is the order of sayings in Marcion's Gospel which he follows.[2]

The contradictions Ritschl has noted are certainly impressive, but they are not decisive. If the Gospels were not yet canonized, as he rightly points out they were not, there is nothing to prevent Justin preferring his own traditional accounts to those given in Luke or any other of the Gospels—assuming that he had even noticed the contradictions. Ritschl's brief discussion of a group of Jesus' sayings in Justin is much more compelling, and it is in this sort of analysis that we shall find the best proof of our case.

Ritschl's discussion of Justin's sources was only one of many which were written within and outside the Tübingen School at that time. Semisch's attempt (1848) to attribute all the discrepancies between Justin and the synoptic Gospels to Justin's poor memory was almost completely discredited, and Credner's thesis (1832) that Justin was using another Gospel source was followed in general by almost everyone, though conservative critics like Zahn (1889) tried to minimize the extent to which this other source had been employed.[3] E. R. Buckley has more recently added a valuable footnote to this discussion by showing that the form of Justin's citations indicates that he was using a source. This "Gospel" differed in contents and order from the synoptic Gospels, which he also quoted.[4]

By drawing on the rich collection of gospel-citations in the

[1] Cf. Hilgenfeld's point (1850) that it is very surprising that Justin, who was a Samaritan, should have never mentioned any of the Samaritan incidents and sayings in Luke.

[2] See the brilliant discussion of Apol. 16.11,12, op. cit., 150f.

[3] See the survey in Wilh. Bousset, *Die Evangeliencitate Justins des Märtyrers in ihrem Wert für die Evangelienkritik* (Göttingen, 1891), Einleitung, 1–9.

[4] E. R. Buckley, "Justin Martyr's Quotations from the Synoptic Tradition", *J.T.S.*, xxxvi (1935), 173–6.

Fathers, Bousset, in the last decade of the nineteenth century, tried to discover more precisely what this other Gospel might be. He came to the conclusion that the source Justin was using for many of his sayings of Jesus was older than the parallels in our Synoptics, and was indeed the collection of the Lord's words used by Matthew and Luke (i.e., Q).

Bousset's seems to have been the last full-scale attempt to argue that Justin's other source material was in any way source material for the canonical Evangelists. The ruling theory to-day is that Justin for the most part relied on a Gospel-harmony. This theory also goes back to the early years of the nineteenth century and took many forms, among which it is interesting to notice Eichhorn's, that the harmony consisted of Matthew enriched by Luke.[1] Sanday in *The Gospels in the Second Century*[2] concluded that Justin either used the canonical Gospels or a harmony of them, inclining to the second alternative. "This, however, does not exclude the possibility", he wrote, "that Justin may at times quote from uncanonical Gospels as well."[3] Sanday has been followed by Lippelt (1901) and Köster (1957).[4]

There are six passages peculiar to Luke's Gospel and one in Acts where the verbal parallel with Justin is almost exact: Luke 1.35,38, Dial. 100.5; Luke 1.31,32, Apol. 33.5; Luke 6.29, Apol. 16.1 (except for the phrase τὸν χιτῶνα ἢ τὸ ἱμάτιον, in which the order is that of Matt.); Luke 18.27, Apol. 19.6; Luke 20.35,36, Dial. 81.4;[5] Luke 23.46, Dial. 105.4 (a quotation

[1] Paulus, Gratz, Storr, and von Engelhardt were among the early advocates of the harmony theory. See Ritschl., op. cit., 139.

[2] London, 1876.

[3] Ibid., 129; cf. 136 n 1.

[4] *Synoptische Überlieferung bei den Apostolischen Vätern*, T.U., 65 (Berlin, 1957), 87–90. Köster promises a full book on the subject, 87 and 267. The harmony theory has recently been condemned by G. Quispel, *Vigiliae Christianae*, xi (1957), 140f. He wishes to return to the theory of Credner and Hilgenfeld, that Justin did not know the four canonical Gospels and used the Gospel of the Hebrews.

[5] Sanday, op. cit., 128, argues that ἰσάγγελοι was coined by Luke to represent ὡς ἄγγελοι in Matt. and Mark, and that Justin could only have taken it from Luke. The fact that a word occurs for the first time in Luke does not prove that Luke coined it.

from Ps. 30.6 (31.5) which differs from the form in the LXX);
Acts 10.42, Dial 118.1 (plus Barn. 7.2; 2 Clem. 1.1; Polyc.
Phil. 2.1; Hegesippus in Eus., *H.E.*, iii.20.4; cf. Acts 17.31;
1 Pet .4.5; 2 Tim. 4.1). The western text of Luke 3.22 is found
in Dial. 103.6.

These agreements cannot be lightly dismissed, but the case
of Acts 10.42, which appears independently in a number of
other early writings besides Justin's Dialogue, shows that Justin
is not necessarily copying from Luke. It is possible that Justin
and Luke are using a common source, and that neither has
made any change in the source in these quotations. (Luke often
changes Mark, the only one of his sources by which we can
check his accuracy, but he does not always do so.) As far as we
can see, none of the verses above which Justin has repeated
bear the marks of Lucan editorial alteration.

In the cases where Justin agrees with Matthew there is little
doubt that Matthew is the source; many of the agreements
contain obvious Matthean editorial work.[1] It is where Justin
seems to be combining material from Matthew with other
material that critics have found reason to believe that the other
source was Luke. In thirteen instances it seems possible to put
this hypothesis to the test.

At the end of the fourteenth chapter of the Apology (the
so-called First Apology), Justin says that he is going "to cite a
few precepts given by the Messiah himself". The next three
chapters contain a whole complex of Jesus' sayings which are of
particular interest to us since, though many appear to be
summaries of Matthew, the rest often differ from Matthew and
converge towards Luke.

Table I shows the parallels to Apol. 15.9,10a in the Dia-
logue, Matthew, Luke, the Didache, and the Latin Didascalia.[2]
The phrase "pray for your enemies" is also found in Apol. 14.3;
Dialogue 35.8; 96.3; Syrian Didascalia v.14 (Connolly, p. 184,

---

[1] Buckley, op. cit., 173 n 1, notes Matt. 17.10–13 quoted in Dial. 49.
[2] R. H. Connolly, *J.T.S.*, xxiv (1923), 147–57 at 148, argues that the
Didascalia is dependent on the Didache. The different order of the clauses
counts against direct dependence.

l.27); Ps. Clem. Hom. xii.32.1 (Behm, p. 190, l.21), and the Oxyrh. Pap. 1224.[1] The frequency with which the phrase occurs by itself, its absence from Luke and the Latin Didascalia parallel, and its position in the Didache (where it looks like an insertion)[2] all suggest that it was a common phrase which would soon find its way into this sort of context.

When we compare Justin and Luke, it is soon clear that Justin is as little dependent on Luke as Luke is on Justin. First, we should expect a harmony of Matthew and Luke to follow the order of one or the other, but Justin's order is unique. Second, in Luke 6.32,33,34 we find the generalized expression "sinners" used to describe the outcasts of society who yet know how to love those who love them. Matthew uses Tax-gatherers in 5.46, the Didache has Gentiles like Matthew in 5.47, while Justin has Adulterers first and Tax-gatherers later. It is unlikely that Justin is dependent on Luke, since the Lucan form looks more like an editorial alteration than do the forms in Justin, nor does he seem to have followed Matthew directly. Third, in the Didache and Luke the formula "what credit (χάρις) is that to you?" appears. The parallel in Justin, "what is distinctive (καινόν) about what you do?", is not taken from Matthew (though cf. Matthew 5.47), and it is hard to see how it could be directly dependent on Luke.

Fourth, because Luke has reproduced the Q-phrase "love your enemies" he is forced to fall back on the weak "do good to those who hate you". "Love those who hate you" is found in the Didache and the Latin Didascalia as well as twice in Justin, and is doubtless original. Justin is not dependent on Luke as he does not reproduce the phrase; indeed, if this case were considered alone, it would be possible to argue that Luke was

---

[1] Köster, op. cit., 221; Bousset, op. cit., 75f. Köster, 220–6, discusses in full the parallels between Did., Matt., and Luke, and concludes, after a tortuous and unconvincing argument, that Did. is dependent on Matt. and Luke (230).

[2] Köster, op. cit., 223f, suggests that it arose in the Church as a reflection on Matt. and Luke (cf. Pol. Phil. 12.3). It may have been a product of ecclesiastical usage, but there is no evidence to suggest that Matt. and Luke provided the basis for its growth.

harmonizing Q and Justin! The comparison at this point is one of the most damaging against the theory that Justin is harmonizing Matthew and Luke.

The second case in which it is possible to test whether Justin is dependent on Luke is in the same chapter of the Apology (15.12a, Table II). Further parallel passages are cited by Köster[1] from 2 Clem. 6.2 and Clem. of Alex., *Strom.*, vi.14. 112.3, but they only confirm what can be deduced from the comparison of Matthew and Luke. Justin is probably giving a shortened version of Matthew in the second part of the section, as he does so often elsewhere in this chapter. In the first part his wording follows Matthew exactly, except at one point. He uses the verb ἀπόλλυμι for Matthew's ζημιόω, while Luke uses both verbs. The alternatives are either that Justin, using Matthew, decided to avoid Matthew's verb here in favour of one of Luke's verbs, or that Luke has harmonized Q with the independent form of the saying preserved in Justin. The second alternative is the more probable, especially as Clement of Alexandria also preserves the saying with ἀπόλλυμι alone.

Justin's treatment of Matthew in the chapter of the Apology we have been considering is almost invariably to abbreviate (e.g. Apology 16.2 is a summary of Matthew 5.22,41,16). If his tendency is to abbreviate, it is unlikely that his longer version of Luke 10.19 in Dialogue 76.6 is dependent on Luke (see Table III). The differences are so marked (Luke: ἰδού, δέδωκα, πατεῖν, omits σκολοπενδρῶν, adds last clause) and the substance so similar that it is almost certain that both writers were using the one source.[2]

A discussion of the various forms in which the famous saying "No one knows the Son except the Father " has been transmitted is not an essential part of our case, since the differences between Justin and Matthew are in no way similar to the

---

[1] Op. cit., 74.
[2] Sanday, op. cit., 125: "The insertion of σκολοπενδρῶν here is curious. It may be perhaps to some extent paralleled by the insertion of καὶ εἰς θήραν in Rom. 11.9." It is easier to explain it as Luke's omission rather than as Justin's addition.

differences between Luke and Matthew (see Table IV). However, it is an excellent example of Justin's use of an independent tradition and it throws light on Marcion's editorial methods.

All the peculiarities in Justin are found elsewhere—the omission of μου; the reversal of the clauses, Father-Son, Son-Father; the plural οἷς; the omission of βούληται.[1] Some of these are found in textual variants to Matthew and Luke, but the important reversal of the clauses is not, and it would be false to assume that the differences between Justin and the Synoptics were due to Justin's use of a poor text. The reversal of the clauses shows that Justin is not dependent on the Synoptics at all; he is reproducing another form of the saying which is found, at least once, in the Pseudo-Clementines, Irenaeus, Origen, Eusebius, Epiphanius, and others.[2] In any case he is not dependent on Luke because he does not reproduce the characteristic Lucan τίς ἐστιν. Justin calls his source "the Gospel".[3]

Marcion is using Luke, since he copies the τίς ἐστιν (Tertull. iv.25). Although the reversal of the clauses makes his own theological point rather better, he is not the originator of the change, as it appears already in Justin and is later reproduced by anti-marcionite writers. Marcion may have been influenced by theological motives—what text-critic is not?—but the problem was not of his own making. It seems that he had in front of him a copy of Luke and a copy of the variant tradition which we can recover from Justin and other sources. The order in Justin, etc., is in some ways more acceptable than the canonical order, in affirming that knowledge of the Son is not confined to the Father, having been revealed to some men by the Son himself. Marcion would have had good critical reasons

[1] Bousset, op. cit., 100–3.
[2] Ps. Clem. xvii.4.3 (Behm, p. 230, ll.27ff); xviii.4.2 (p. 243, ll.2ff;) the Marcosians cited by Iren. i.13.2 (Harvey i.180); iv.11.2 (v. l.) (Harvey ii.159); Iren. ii.4.5 (Harvey i.263); Origen, De princ., ii.6.1; Eus., Dem. Ev., iv.3.13; v.1.25f; De eccles. theol., i.12.7; H.E., i.2.2; Epiph., Anc., 11.3; 19.7; 67.5; Haer, 34.18.16; 74.4.5, etc.
[3] Dial. 100.1, καὶ ἐν τῷ εὐαγγελίῳ δὲ γέγραπται εἰπών. See Buckley, op. cit., 175.

for emending the text of Luke; he was not trying to recover the best text of Luke, but the best text of the original "Gospel".

In the command to love God and love thy neighbour (see Table V), Justin's Dialogue shares two important peculiarities with Luke: the phrase "with all thy strength"[1] and the passing from the first part to the second without a break. It is, of course, possible that Justin twice omitted the "soul" and "mind" phrases in harmonizing Matthew and Luke, but it is far more likely that Luke is the harmonizer. Luke seems to have edited the tradition he shared with Justin in the light of Q, which was his source for the phrases "with all thy soul" and "with all thy mind". The parallel in the Apology shows the influence of another part of Matthew on Justin (Matt. 4.10), and is the first indication we have struck that Justin may have been composing his own harmony as he went along, sometimes harmonizing his tradition with Matthew and sometimes not.

The woe on those who tithe has been transmitted in two recensions, the "dill and cumin" version in Matthew and the "rue" version in Justin and Luke. Although Justin and Luke both witness to the non-Matthean version, neither is dependent on the other (see Table VI). The different position occupied by the "judgement" in each of them suggests that they have edited their common tradition differently in the light of Matthew (and Q). If Justin was harmonizing Luke with Matthew, it is more likely that he would have put the "love of God" clause in Luke's position. Luke's phrase "and every herb" looks more like an editorial harmonization than Justin's omission of everything except "rue".

The woe against those who have the keys and yet shut men out (see Table VII) is obviously taken from a common non-Matthean tradition by both Justin and Luke. Luke has two peculiarities which Justin does not follow: νομικός instead of γραμματεύς and the "key of knowledge" for "the keys". The former may be a Lucan editorial change, as only Luke uses

---

[1] Cf. Deut. 6.5, LXX, which has "heart", "soul", and "strength" (δυνάμεως); it does not, however, seem to have played a direct part in the formation of Luke or Justin's versions.

the word νομικός in the Gospels (except for Matt. 22.35);[1] the latter almost certainly is. The change from Justin's form to Luke's is easy to imagine, but it is much harder to see why Justin should change "key" to "keys", even if he wished to suppress the reference to Gnosis.[2]

In the saying "fear those who can cast you into Gehenna" (see Table VIII), it is most unlikely that Justin is dependent on Luke. The saying is preserved in at least two forms, and Matthew is clearly one of them. Matthew has at least three features which are absent in all the others or only present in one or two of them: φοβεῖσθε (lines 1 and 11); ἀποκτεῖναι (line 8); ἀπολέσαι (line 16). The words which stand in place of these four are sufficiently similar for us to assume that they come from one source and not more than one source. All the features which are also found in Matthew are underlined in the other five columns of the Table, and we may assume that some at least are due to the influence of Matthew or Matthew's source Q. Marcion is the writer who shows the least traces of Matthean influence: ἀπό (line 2), ἀποκτέννειν (line 3), and possibly δυναμένων (line 4). Marcion, however, is dependent on Luke, reproducing Luke's introductory formula, "I say to (you my) friends" (not in the Table), his central bridge-passage (lines 9 and 10), and his conclusion. Since there is no discernible theological purpose at work, we may at least ask whether again he is not emending Luke in the light of another tradition which he believes to be more ancient.

Köster has tentatively suggested that 2 Clement, Justin, and the Pseudo Clementine Homilies are here following a common Gospel-harmony, that is, of Matthew and Luke.[3] If Luke is the

---

[1] See G. D. Kilpatrick, *J.T.S.*, N.S., i (1950), 56–60.

[2] The Gospel according to Thomas provides additional evidence for a tradition containing the plural "keys"; it follows Luke in reading "of knowledge" and Matthew in referring to "the Pharisees" as well as to "the Scribes": plate 88, lines 7 to 10 (Logion 39 in the edition of A. Guillaumont, H.-Ch. Puech, G. Quispel, W. Till, and Yassah 'Abd Al Masîḥ, Leiden and London, 1959): "The Pharisees and the Scribes have received the keys of Knowledge, they have hidden them. They did not enter, and they did not let those (enter) who wished."

[3] Op. cit., 94–7.

other source employed by 2 Clem., Justin, and Ps. Clem., it is
hard to see why all have omitted ὑποδείξω, etc. (lines 9 and 10),
why 2 Clem. and Justin omit ἀπό (line 2) and τὸ σῶμα (line 3),
and why 2 Clem. and Ps. Clem. add πυρός (lines 17 and 18).
Each of these separately might be explained away, but together they make it unlikely that they are dependent directly
on Luke. If they are all using a Gospel-harmony it is again
difficult to explain why they differ from each other and adopt
different words from Matthew (e.g. lines 1 and 14).

The only hypothesis left is to suppose that all five were
acquainted with another recension of the saying, which each
has harmonized in his own way with Matthew or Q. Marcion is
perhaps the nearest to the original. The distinguishing marks
of this source were that it made no reference to "body and
soul" and that it specifically mentioned the ἐξουσία of the
opponent Christians must fear.

The parallels to Apol. 16.9–11 have been adduced to prove that
Justin was employing a harmony of Matthew and Luke.[1] The
case rests on the phrase (Table IX, column iii, line 9) in Apol.
16.10, καὶ ποιεῖ ἃ λέγω, which is a variant of a phrase in Luke
6.46. As can be seen from the Table, Justin has followed
Matthew's wording in the "Lord, Lord" saying. The supposition
is that, using a harmony of Matthew and Luke, he observed that
the Lucan parallel to Matthew contained an extra phrase.
This extra phrase fitted neatly into the next saying, "He who
hears me, etc.", and there he put it.

Three comments should be made. First, if this hypothesis is
correct, the supposed harmony would probably have been in
the nature of a synopsis, since Justin has adopted the extra
phrase in Apol. 16.10 and chosen not to adopt it in Apol. 63.5;
the phrase had not been completely harmonized in Justin's
source. Second, there is no evidence that it was Luke which
Justin was harmonizing with Matthew. The evidence goes the
other way. The saying in Apol. 16.10 and 63.5 is not found in
the best text of Luke; it is substituted for the last clause of Luke
10.16 by D and some codices of the Old Latin, added to the

[1] Köster, op. cit., 87–90.

usual text by Θ, family 13, some codices of the Old Latin and
two Syriac versions and, in an earlier position, by Ps. Ign. Eph.,
Cyprian, etc.[1] From the fact that it is lodged in three different
ways we should deduce that it was another tradition attracted
to Luke 10.16 early in the history of the text.[2] If Justin had been
working from a "Western" text of Luke, he would almost
certainly have reproduced more of verse 16.

Third, the general character of the context of the sayings in
Justin should be taken into account. This is part of the collection of the Lord's sayings which began in chapter 14 of the
Apology. As the simplified list given here shows, the Apology
provides a continuity which is paralleled now by Matthew,
now by Luke.

| Matthew | Apology | Luke |
|---------|---------|------|
| 7.21 | 16.9 | (6.46) |
| | 16.10 | (10.16: D, etc.) |
| 7.22f | 16.11 | 13.26f |
| 13.42f | 16.12 | 13.28 |
| 7.15 | 16.13 | |

On grounds of *order*, it is easier to suppose that Matthew and
Luke have followed a collection of sayings with Justin's order
than that Justin has jumped hither and thither in Matthew and
Luke to compile a harmonized collection. When we turn to the
*wording* we find that Justin's wording is mainly Matthean, but
that occasionally a phrase which is also found in Luke appears.
Apology 16.11 (cf. Dialogue 76.5) is an instructive example.
For the most part it follows Matthew 7.22f, but it includes the
words, ἐφάγομεν καὶ ἐπίομεν, which should be compared with
Luke 13.26, ἐφάγομεν ἐνώπιόν σου καὶ ἐπίομεν. It is possible
that Justin has harmonized Matthew with Luke, but the fact
that he does not reproduce the Lucanism, ἐνώπιόν σου,[3] reinforces the conclusion we have reached in other passages that
Justin harmonized an unknown source with Matthew, and that
Luke independently employed the same source.

---

[1] Bousset, op. cit., 86f.   [2] Bousset's conclusion.
[3] Hawkins, *Horae Synopticae* (2nd ed., Oxford, 1909), 18.

On these three grounds it is unlikely that Justin was here using a Gospel-harmony of Matthew and Luke, or that the harmony he made as he went along was based on Luke.

In the dialogue between Jesus and the rich man, Justin is independent of Matthew (Table X). He has no trace of Matthew's "Why do you ask me concerning the good?" The question is whether Justin has used Luke.

First, his omission of the rest of the rich man's question may not be simply the abbreviation of a source which originally contained it. There is independent evidence that other accounts of the incident had separated versions of the two parts of the question. The Marcosians (Iren. i.13.1; Harvey i.178) seem to have preserved the question and answer in exactly the words of the Dialogue version, without the second part of the question about eternal life, and the Gospel according to the Hebrews (Origen, *Comm. in Matt.* xv.14; Klostermann, p. 389, ll.21ff) preserves the second part of the question separately, ascribing it to "another rich man" (*dixit ad eum alter divitum*).[1] Justin's omission of the question about eternal life may be due to a peculiarity of his source.

Second, although the wording in the Dialogue contains Jesus' counter-question in the form found in Luke (and Mark), and the statement "One is good" is like Matthew, it is very unlikely that Justin is dependent on either of them. The reason is that not only the Marcosians' tradition cited above but also the Gospel of the Naasseni (Hippol., *Philos.* v.7.26) preserves exactly the same wording; it is unlikely that three writers would arrive independently at a wording which, although it contained phrases found in Matthew and Luke, also contained an identical ending not found elsewhere.

Third, Marcion seems to have used a form of the independent tradition preserved in the Dialogue to edit Luke (Marcion according to Epiphanius, Schol. 50). His μή με λέγε ἀγαθὸν is

---

[1] Bousset, op. cit., 106, produces a text of the Gospel according to the Hebrews which contains the question of the *first* rich man (with a form of Jesus' answer like Marcion's), but I have been unable to trace his source.

supported by Ps. Clem. Hom. xviii.1.3; cf. 3.4: μή με λέγε ἀγαθὸν ὁ γὰρ ἀγαθὸς εἷς ἐστιν ὁ πατὴρ ὁ ἐν τοῖς οὐρανοῖς.

Fourth, the form of the question and answer preserved in the Apology is close to Luke (and Mark), but the differences are still great enough to make it impossible to affirm that Luke (or Mark) has been used. Justin does not give Jesus' counter question, and he has μόνος ὁ θεός ὁ ποίησας τὰ πάντα instead of εἷς (ὁ) θεὸς. The latter difference may be an anti-Marcionite alteration, but dependence on Luke (or Mark) cannot be proved.

Justin's version of the eucharistic words is closer to Luke and Paul than to Matthew or Mark, but is independent of any of them (see Table XI). This is clear from the order of the "remembrance" phrase over the bread and the omission of any reference to the covenant over the cup. It is incredible that a harmonizer should have omitted so much or changed the order of the parts. The extraordinary thing is that these words, dependent directly on none of our Gospels or Paul, are contained in a passage where Justin claims to be quoting from "the memoirs of the Apostles called Gospels". We are forced to conclude that his other source (whether a Gospel ascribed to the Apostles, or his own Church's eucharistic tradition) is just as authoritative for him as Matthew, the only canonical Gospel we can be sure he possessed.

Justin claims that the tradition about Christ's agony in Gethsemane[1] when he sweated drops of blood is also taken from the memoirs of the Apostles (see Table XII). Here, however, Justin adds that the memoirs were written by those who followed the Apostles as well as by the Apostles themselves.[2] This has been taken to be a specific reference to Luke 1.1,3, and the fact that only Luke records the drops of blood is supposed to clinch the case that Justin used Luke. A number of considerations makes this unlikely. The words about those who followed the Apostles need not refer to Luke, and they could equally well apply to Mark or to any other Gospel which

[1] Note that both Justin and Luke omit all reference to Gethsemane as the scene of the agony (Luke 22.40; Dial. 99.2; 103.8).

[2] Dial 103.8: ἐν τοῖς ἀπομνημονεύμασι, ἅ φημι ὑπὸ τῶν ἀποστόλων αὐτοῦ καὶ τῶν ἐκείνοις παρακολουθησάντων συντετάχθαι.

could not claim direct apostolic authorship. If Justin particularly wished to direct attention to Luke's Gospel, he would surely have quoted from it exactly. Earlier in the Dialogue (99.2) he has quoted the words "Let this cup pass from me" almost exactly from Matthew; on the later occasion when he is supposed to be specifically quoting from Luke his version differs greatly: he omits πάτερ and ἀπ' ἐμοῦ, and he adopts neither of the Lucan pecularities, βούλει and παρένεγκε. Perhaps, however, these differences are due to abbreviation and harmonization with Matthew, so we must turn to the words about sweating drops of blood where, according to the theory we are criticizing, he had only Luke on which to rely.

The first thing to notice is that it is by no means certain that Luke 22.44 stood in Luke at all. It is included by ℵ* D Θ 0171 f1 157, etc., Latin, Syriac Curetonian and Peshitta, and Armenian, and omitted by a corrector of ℵ, A B W f13, etc., f, Syriac Sinaiticus, and Sahidic. Family 13 omits it in Luke and puts it after Matt. 26.39. If Justin proves to be a witness to a separate tradition, we should have another example of the extra-canonical source giving rise to textual variants in the canonical Gospels.[1] But to assume that would be to assume what we have to prove. We can only leave open the question of whether Justin's text of Luke, supposing he knew Luke, contained this verse.

The most important difference between Justin's citation and Luke is the order; in Luke, the prayer precedes the agony and in Justin it follows. Justin does not have αἵματος after θρόμβοι, has κατεχεῖτο instead of καταβαίνοντες, and omits "upon earth". If there is any dependence of one upon the other, it is slightly more likely that the Lucan text is dependent on Justin; it is more likely that the additional words are the result of editorial expansion than that they are the result of editorial shortening. The differences are too great for this passage to be used to show that Justin was quoting from Luke.[2] Taking all the uncertainties into account, there is a good case for arguing that the verse did not originally belong to Luke and that it

[1] Cf. Matt. 7.22 syr^c, Table IX.
[2] Sanday, op. cit., 124, holds that the opposite is true.

was inserted into his text from the tradition which Justin quotes, "the Apostles' Memoirs".

The three predictions of the passion in Justin are so similar that they probably all come from the one source (see Table XIII). That source may have been a harmony of Matthew and Luke, or it may have been an independent tradition. Matthew seems to have exerted no special influence; none of its special features appears in Justin, and anything else they have in common is also found in Luke. The only remaining possibility is that Justin's source is a harmony of the two predictions in Luke. (The other predictions in Matthew and Luke show no particular affinities; this in itself raises the problem of why Justin did not draw on a wider range of sources for his harmony, if he was making a harmony; Matthew 17.22f; Luke 9.44; Matthew 20.18f; Luke 18.31–3.) It is unlikely that he should harmonize by choosing to name only one of the groups which rejected Jesus, the scribes, out of the three available, and then add to them the Pharisees. It is very likely that Justin reproduced an old source which was independent of the canonical Gospels.

The few remaining passages where there are verbal points of contact between Justin and Luke are such that it is impossible to tell whether Justin was dependent on Luke. None of them repeats Lucan passages which are obviously editorial additions, and three of them occur in Justin's collections of sayings which we have argued could not, at other points, have been dependent on Luke. These passages are: Luke 5.32, Apol. 15.8, where Justin goes on to record a non-canonical saying about repentance; Luke 12.48, Apol. 17.4: "to whom much is given"; and, from the collection in Apol. 15 and 16: Luke 5.35,36, Apol. 15.13, Dial. 96.3;[1] one phrase in Luke 13.26, Apol. 16.11, Dial. 76.5; Luke 13.28, Apol. 16.12; Luke 6.44, Apol. 16.13.

To conclude, the evidence is certainly not strong enough to prove that Justin used Luke's Gospel. There is much to show that Luke employed Justin's special source; that is the simplest hypothesis to explain all the facts.

[1] Bousset, op. cit., 80–3.

TABLE I

| Matt. 5.46,44,42 | Justin. Apol.15.9,10a | Justin Dial.133.6 | Didache 1.3,5 | Didascalia (latin) i.2.3 (Connolly,pp.11,12) | Lk.6.32f-27f,30,34 |
|---|---|---|---|---|---|
| 26. ἐὰν γὰρ ἀγαπήσητε τ.ἀγαπῶντας ὑμᾶς τίνα μισθὸν ἔχετε; οὐχὶ κ.οἱ τελῶναι τ.αὐτὸ ποιοῦσιν; 44 ἐγὼ δὲ λέγω ὑμῖν ἀγαπᾶτε τ.ἐχθροὺς ὑμῶν | 9c. εἰ ἀγαπᾶτε τ.ἀγαπῶντας ὑμᾶς τί καινὸν ποιεῖτε; κ.εἰ γὰρ οἱ πόρνοι τοῦτο ποιοῦσιν 10a ἐγὼ δὲ ὑμῖν λέγω | | 3 ποία γὰρ χάρις ἐὰν ἀγαπᾶτε τ.ἀγαπῶντας ὑμᾶς; οὐχὶ κ.τ.ἔθνη τ.αὐτὸ ποιοῦσιν; | | 32. εἰ ἀγαπᾶτε τ.ἀγαπῶντας ὑμᾶς ποία ὑμῖν χάρις ἐστίν... κ.οἱ ἁμαρτωλοὶ 33... κ.οἱ ἁμαρτωλοὶ |
| | εὔχεσθε ὑπὲρ τ.ἐχθρῶν ὑμῶν κ.ἀγαπᾶτε τ.μισοῦντας ὑμᾶς κ.εὐλογεῖτε κ.καταρωμένους ὑμῖν κ.εὔχεσθε ὑπὲρ τ.ἐπηρεαζόντων ὑμᾶς | 85.7 ἀγαπᾶν κ.τ.ἐχθροὺς εὔχεσθε κ. ὑπὲρ τ.ἐχθρῶν κ.ἀγαπᾶν τ.μισοῦντας κ.εὐλογεῖν τ.καταρωμένους | [κ.προσεύχεσθε ὑπὲρ τ.ἐχθρῶν ὑμῶν] ὑμεῖς δὲ ἀγαπᾶτε τ.μισοῦντας ὑμᾶς κ.εὐλογεῖτε τ.καταρωμένους ὑμῖν κ.προσεύχεσθε ὑπὲρ τ. ἐχθρῶν ὑμῶν νηστεύετε δὲ ὑπὲρ τ.διωκόντων ὑμᾶς | diligite oblentes vos & ouria pro maledicentibus vos | 27. τ.ἀγαπῶντας ὑμᾶς κ.καλῶς ποιεῖτε τ.μισοῦσιν ὑμᾶς 28.εὐλογεῖτε τ.καταρωμένους ὑμᾶς προσεύχεσθε περὶ τ. ἐπηρεαζόντων ὑμᾶς |
| καὶ προσεύχεσθε | | | | | |
| ὑπὲρ τ.διωκόντων ὑμᾶς | | | κ.οὐχ ἕξετε ἐχθρόν | & inimicum nullum habebitis | |
| 42. τ.αἰτοῦντί σε δὸς κ.τ.θέλοντα | 10a. παντὶ τ.αἰτοῦντι δίδοτε κ.π̄ βουλόμενον | | 5 παντὶ τ.αἰτοῦντί σε δίδου | | 30. παντὶ αἰτοῦντί σε δίδου κ.ἀπὸ τ.αἴροντος τὰ σὰ μὴ ἀπαίτει |
| ἀπὸ σοῦ δανείσασθαι μὴ ἀποστραφῇς | δανείσασθαι μὴ ἀποστραφῆτε εἰ γὰρ δανείζετε παρ'ὧν ἐλπίζετε λαβεῖν τί καινὸν ποιεῖτε; τοῦτο κ.οἱ τελῶναι ποιοῦσιν | | κ.μὴ ἀπαίτει | | 34. κ.ἐὰν δανείσητε παρ'ὧν ἐλπίζετε λαβεῖν ποία ὑμῖν χάρις ἐστίν; κ.ἁμαρτωλοὶ ἁμαρτωλοῖς δανείζουσιν ἵνα ἀπολάβωσιν τ.ἴσα |

## TABLE II

| Matt. 16.26 | Justin Apol. 15.12a | Lk. 9.25 |
|---|---|---|
| τί γὰρ ὠφεληθήσεται ἄνθρωπος ἐὰν τ. κόσμον ὅλον κερδήσῃ τ. δὲ ψυχὴν αὐτοῦ<br><br>ζημιωθῇ; *<br>ἢ τί δώσει ἄνθρωπος ἀντάλλαγμα τ. ψυχῆς αὐτοῦ; | τί γὰρ ὠφελεῖται ἄνθρωπος ἂν τ. κόσμον ὅλον κερδήσῃ τ. δὲ ψυχὴν αὐτοῦ ἀπολέσῃ; †<br><br>ἢ τί δώσει αὐτῆς ἀντάλλαγμα; | τί γὰρ ὠφελεῖται ἄνθρωπος κερδήσας τ. κόσμον ὅλον ἑαυτὸν δὲ ἀπολέσας ἢ ζημιωθείς; |
| * cf. II Clem. 6.2. | † cf. Clem. Alex. Strom. VI.xiv.112.3 | |

## TABLE III

| Justin Dial. 76.6 | Lk. 10.19 |
|---|---|
| δίδωμι ὑμῖν ἐξουσίαν καταπατεῖν ἐπάνω ὄφεων κ. σκορπίων κ. σκολοπενδρῶν κ. ἐπάνω πάσης δυνάμεως τ. ἐχθροῦ | ἰδοὺ δέδωκα ὑμῖν τ. ἐξουσίαν τοῦ πατεῖν ἐπάνω ὄφεων κ. σκορπίων κ. ἐπὶ πᾶσαν τ. δύναμιν τ. ἐχθροῦ κ. οὐδὲν ὑμᾶς οὐ μὴ ἀδικήσει |

TABLE IV

| Matt. 11.27 | Justin Dial. 100.1 | Marcion<br>Harnack 2.ed., 206* | Lk. 10.22 |
|---|---|---|---|
| πάντα μοι παρεδόθη<br>ὑπὸ τοῦ πατρός μου<br>κ. οὐδεὶς ἐπιγνώσκει<br>τ. υἱὸν<br>εἰ μὴ ὁ πατήρ<br>οὐδὲ τ. πατέρα<br>τις ἐπιγνώσκει<br>εἰ μὴ ὁ υἱὸς<br>κ. ᾧ ἐὰν βούληται<br>ὁ υἱὸς ἀποκαλύψαι | πάντα μοι παραδέδοται<br>ὑπὸ τοῦ πατρός<br>κ. οὐδεὶς γινώσκει<br>τ. πατέρα<br>εἰ μὴ ὁ υἱὸς<br>οὐδὲ τ. υἱὸν<br><br>εἰ μὴ ὁ πατήρ<br>κ. οἷς ἂν<br>ὁ υἱὸς ἀποκαλύψῃ | πάντα μοι παρεδόθη<br>ὑπὸ τοῦ πατρός<br>(κ)οὐδεὶς γινώσκει (ἔγνω?)<br>τίς ἐστιν ὁ πατήρ<br>εἰ μὴ ὁ υἱὸς<br>κ. τίς ἐστιν ὁ υἱὸς<br><br>εἰ μὴ ὁ πατήρ<br>κ. ᾧ ἐὰν<br>ὁ υἱὸς ἀποκαλύψῃ | πάντα μοι παρεδόθη<br>ὑπὸ τοῦ πατρός μου<br>κ. οὐδεὶς γινώσκει<br>τίς ἐστιν ὁ υἱὸς<br>εἰ μὴ ὁ πατήρ<br>κ. τίς ἐστιν ὁ πατήρ<br><br>εἰ μὴ ὁ υἱὸς<br>κ. ᾧ ἐὰν βούληται<br>ὁ υἱὸς ἀποκαλύψαι |

TABLE V

| Matt.22.37-9 [4.10] | Justin Apol.16.6 | Justin Dial.93.2 | Didache 1.2 | Lk.10.27 |
|---|---|---|---|---|
| [cf. 22.38] [4.10] [κύριον τ. θεόν σου προσκυνήσεις κ. αὐτῷ μόνῳ λατρεύσεις] 37ἀγαπήσεις κύριον τ. θεόν σου ἐν ὅλῃ τ. καρδίᾳ σου κ. ἐν ὅλῃ τ. ψυχῇ σου κ. ἐν ὅλῃ τ. διανοίᾳ σου 38αὕτη ἐστὶν ἡ μεγάλη κ. πρώτη ἐντολή 39δευτέρα ὁμοία αὐτῇ ἀγαπήσεις τ. πλησίον σου ὡς σεαυτόν | μεγίστη τῇ ἐντολή ἐστι κύριον τ. θεόν σου προσκυνήσεις καὶ αὐτῷ μόνῳ λατρεύσεις ἐξ ὅλης τ. καρδίας σου κ. ἐξ ὅλης τ. ἰσχύος σου κύριον τ. θεόν τ. ποιήσαντά σε | [=Dial.103.6] ἀγαπήσεις κύριον τ. θεόν σου ἐξ ὅλης τ. καρδίας σου κ. ἐξ ὅλης τ. ἰσχύος σου κ. τ. πλησίον σου ὡς σεαυτόν =Dial.93.3 (om.σου x4) | πρῶτον ἀγαπήσεις τ. θεόν τ. ποιήσαντά σε * δεύτερον τ. πλησίον σου ὡς σεαυτόν *cf. Barn.19.2 | ἀγαπήσεις κύριον τ. θεόν σου ἐξ ὅλης τ. καρδίας σου κ. ἐν ὅλῃ τ. ψυχῇ σου κ. ἐν ὅλῃ τ. ἰσχύϊ σου κ. ἐν ὅλῃ τ. διανοίᾳ σου κ. τ. πλησίον σου ὡς σεαυτόν |

## TABLE VI

| Matt. 23. 23 | Justin Dial. 17. 3 | Lk. 11. 42 |
|---|---|---|
| οὐαὶ ὑμῖν | οὐαὶ ὑμῖν | ἀλλὰ οὐαὶ ὑμῖν |
| γραμματεῖς κ. φαρισαῖοι | γραμματεῖς κ. φαρισαῖοι | τ. φαρισαίοις |
| ὑποκριταί    ὅτι | ὑποκριταί    ὅτι | ὅτι |
| ἀποδεκατοῦτε τ. ἡδύοσμον | ἀποδεκατοῦτε τ. ἡδύοσμον | ἀποδεκατοῦτε τ. ἡδύοσμον |
| κ. τ. ἄνηθον | κ. τ. πήγανον | κ. τ. πήγανον |
| κ. τ. κύμινον κ. | | κ. πᾶν λάχανον κ. |
| ἀφήκατε τ. βαρύτερα τ. νόμου | | παρέρχεσθε |
| τ. κρίσιν | τ. δὲ ἀγάπην τ. θεοῦ | τ. κρίσιν |
| | κ. τ. κρίσιν | κ. τ. ἀγάπην τ. θεοῦ |
| κ. τ. ἔλεος | | |
| κ. τ. πίστιν | | |
| | οὐ κατανοεῖτε | |

## TABLE VII

| Matt. 23. 13 | Justin Dial. 17. 4 | Lk. 11. 52 |
|---|---|---|
| οὐαὶ δὲ ὑμῖν | οὐαὶ ὑμῖν | οὐαὶ ὑμῖν |
| γραμματεῖς κ. φαρισαῖοι | γραμματεῖς | τ. νομικοῖς |
| ὑποκριταί    ὅτι | ὅτι | ὅτι |
| | τὰς κλεῖς ἔχετε | ἤρατε τὴν κλεῖδα τ. γνώσεως |
| κλείετε | | |
| τ. βασιλείαν τ. οὐρανῶν | | |
| ἔμπροσθεν τ. ἀνθρώπων | | |
| ὑμεῖς γὰρ οὐκ εἰσέρχεσθε | κ. αὐτοὶ οὐκ εἰσέρχεσθε | αὐτοὶ οὐκ εἰσήλθατε |
| οὐδὲ τ. εἰσερχομένους | κ. τ. εἰσερχομένους | κ. τ. εἰσερχομένους |
| ἀφίετε εἰσελθεῖν | κωλύετε | ἐκωλύσατε |
| [23. 16, 24 ὁδηγοὶ τυφλοί] | ὁδηγοὶ τυφλοί | |

TABLE VIII

| Matt. 10.28 | II Clem. 5.4 | Justin Apol. 19.7 | B. Clem. Hom.xvii.5.2 | Marcion, Harnack, 2nd ed. 211f. | Lk. 12.4,5 |
|---|---|---|---|---|---|
| κ. μὴ φοβεῖσθε ἀπὸ τῶν ἀποκτεννόντων τ. σῶμα τ. δὲ ψυχὴν μὴ δυναμένων ἀποκτεῖναι | κ. ὑμεῖς μὴ φοβεῖσθε τοὺς ἀποκτεννοντας ὑμᾶς καὶ μηδὲν ὑμῖν δυναμένους ποιεῖν | μὴ φοβεῖσθε τοὺς ἀναιροῦντας ὑμᾶς κ. μετὰ ταῦτα μὴ δυναμένους τι ποιῆσαι εἶπε | μὴ φοβηθῆτε ἀπὸ τοῦ ἀποκτεννοντος τ. σῶμα τ. δὲ ψυχῇ_ μὴ δυναμένου τι ποιῆσαι | μὴ φοβηθῆτε ἀπὸ τῶν ὑμᾶς μόνον ἀποκτέννειν δυναμένων κ. μετὰ ταῦτα μηδεμίαν εἰς ὑμᾶς ἐχόντων ἐξουσίαν | μὴ φοβηθῆτε ἀπὸ τῶν ἀποκτεννόντων τ. σῶμα κ. μετὰ ταῦτα μὴ ἐχόντων περισσότερόν τι ποιῆσαι |
| φοβεῖσθε δὲ μᾶλλον | ἀλλὰ φοβεῖσθε τὸν μετ. τ.ἀποθανεῖν ὑμᾶς | φοβήθητε δὲ τὸν μετὰ τ.ἀποθανεῖν | φοβήθητε δὲ τὸν | ὑποδείξω δὲ ὑμῖν τίνα φοβήθητε φοβήθητε τον μετ.τ.ἀποκτεῖναι | ὑποδείξω δὲ ὑμῖν τίνα φοβηθῆτε φοβήθητε τον μετὰ τ.ἀποκτεῖναι |
| τὸν δυνάμενον κ. ψυχὴν κ. σῶμα ἀπολέσαι ἐν γεέννῃ | ἔχοντα ἐξουσίαν ψυχῆς κ. σώματος τοῦ βαλεῖν εἰς γέεννα τοῦ πυρός | δυνάμενον κ. ψυχὴν κ. σῶμα εἰς γέενναν ἐμβαλεῖν | δυνάμενον κ. σῶμα κ. ψυχὴν εἰς τ. γέενναν τ. πυρὸς βαλεῖν ναὶ λέγω ὑμῖν τοῦτον φοβήθητε | ἔχοντα ἐξουσίαν βαλεῖν εἰς γέενναν ναὶ λέγω ὑμῖν τοῦτον φοβήθητε | ἔχοντα ἐξουσίαν ἐμβαλεῖν εἰς τ. γέενναν ναὶ λέγω ὑμῖν τοῦτον φοβήθητε |

underlining: possible influence of Matt., Q marcion.

TABLE IX

| Matt. 7.21 | II Clem. 4.2 | Justin Apol. 16.9f. | Justin Apol. 63.5 | Lk. 6.46; [10.16*] |
|---|---|---|---|---|
| οὐ πᾶς ὁ λέγων μοι κύριε κύριε εἰσελεύσεται εἰς τ. βασιλείαν τ. οὐρανῶν | οὐ πᾶς ὁ λέγων μοι κύριε κύριε σωθήσεται | ⁹ οὐχὶ πᾶς ὁ λέγων μοι κύριε κύριε εἰσελεύσεται εἰς τ. βασιλείαν τ. οὐρανῶν | | 6.46 Τί δέ με καλεῖτε κύριε κύριε |
| ἀλλ' ὁ ποιῶν τ. θέλημα τ. πατρός μου τοῦ ἐν τ. οὐρανοῖς | ἀλλ' ὁ ποιῶν τ. δικαιοσύνην | ἀλλ' ὁ ποιῶν τ. θέλημα τ. πατρός μου τοῦ ἐν τ. οὐρανοῖς | | κ. οὐ ποιεῖτε ἃ λέγω; |
| | | 10ᵃ ὃς γὰρ ἀκούει μου κ. ποιεῖ ἃ λέγω ἀκούει | ὁ ἐμοῦ ἀκούων | [10.16*] κ. ὁ ἐμοῦ ἀκούων (cf. 6.46 above) ἀκούει |
| | | τ. ἀποστείλαντός με | ἀκούει τ. ἀποστείλαντός με | τ. ἀποστείλαντός με |
| | | | | add [10.16*] Θ f13 a b syᶜ cf. D i l r |

TABLE X

| Matt. 19.16.f | Justin Dial. 101.2 | Justin Apol. 16.7 | Marcion Epiph. cf Harnack² 225f. | Lk.18.18f (cf. Mk.10.17f.) |
|---|---|---|---|---|
| διδάσκαλε<br>τί ἀγαθὸν ποιήσω<br>ἵνα σχῶ<br>ζωὴν αἰώνιον;<br>ὁ δὲ εἶπεν αὐτῷ<br>τί με ἐρωτᾶς<br>περὶ τ. ἀγαθοῦ;<br>εἷς ἐστιν ὁ ἀγαθός | διδάσκαλε ἀγαθέ<br><br>ἀπεκρίνατο<br>τί με λέγεις<br>ἀγαθόν;<br>εἷς ἐστιν ἀγαθός<br><br>ὁ πατήρ μου<br>ὁ ἐν τ. οὐρανοῖς | διδάσκαλε ἀγαθέ<br><br>ἀπεκρίνατο λέγων<br><br>οὐδεὶς ἀγαθός<br>εἰ μὴ μόνος ὁ θεός<br>ὁ ποιήσας τ. πάντα | διδάσκαλε ἀγαθέ<br>τί ποιήσας<br>ζωὴν αἰώνιον<br>κληρονομήσω;<br>ὁ δὲ<br>μή με λέγε<br>ἀγαθόν<br>εἷς ἐστιν ἀγαθός<br><br>ὁ θεός<br><br>ὁ πατήρ | διδάσκαλε ἀγαθέ<br>τί ποιήσας<br>ζωὴν αἰώνιον<br>κληρονομήσω;<br>εἶπεν δὲ αὐτῷ ὁ Ἰησοῦς<br>τί με λέγεις<br>ἀγαθόν;<br><br>οὐδεὶς ἀγαθός<br>εἰ μὴ εἷς [ὁ] θεός |
| | = Marcosians:<br>Iren. i.3.1 (Harvey i.7f.)<br>τί με...οὐρανοῖς =<br>Gospel Naasseni in<br>Hippol. v.7.26. | | cf. Ps.Clem.Hom.XVIII.1,3.34. | cf. Marcion:<br>Adamantius,<br>Dial. i.1; ii.17<br>Origen,<br>de princ.ii.5.1. |

TABLE XI

| Matt. 26.26-28 | Justin Apol. 66,3 | Lk. 22.19-20 | I Cor. 11.23-25 |
|---|---|---|---|
| ²⁶ ...λαβὼν ὁ Ἰησοῦς ἄρτον<br>κ. εὐλογήσας<br>ἔκλασεν κ. δοὺς τ. μαθηταῖς<br>εἶπεν<br>λάβετε φάγετε | τ. Ἰησοῦν λαβόντα ἄρτον<br>εὐχαριστήσαντα<br><br>εἰπεῖν | ¹⁹ κ. λαβὼν ἄρτον<br>εὐχαριστήσας<br>ἔκλασεν κ. ἔδωκεν αὐτοῖς<br>λέγων | ²³ ...ἔλαβεν ἄρτον<br>²⁴ κ. εὐχαριστήσας<br>ἔκλασεν καὶ<br>εἶπεν |
| τοῦτό ἐστιν τ. σῶμά μου | τοῦτο ποιεῖτε<br>εἰς τ. ἀνάμνησίν μου<br>τοῦτ' ἐστι τ. σῶμά μου | τοῦτό ἐστιν τ. σῶμά μου<br>τ. ὑπὲρ ὑμῶν διδόμενον<br>τοῦτο ποιεῖτε<br>εἰς τ. ἐμὴν ἀνάμνησιν | τοῦτό μού ἐστιν τ. σῶμα<br>τ. ὑπὲρ ὑμῶν<br>τοῦτο ποιεῖτε<br>εἰς τ. ἐμὴν ἀνάμνησιν |
| ²⁷ κ. λαβὼν ποτήριον | κ.τ. ποτήριον ὁμοίως λαβόντα<br>κ. εὐχαριστήσαντα<br>εἰπεῖν | ²⁰ κ.τ. ποτήριον ὡσαύτως<br>μετὰ τ. δειπνῆσαι<br>λέγων | ὡσαύτως κ. τ. ποτήριον<br>μετὰ τ. δειπνῆσαι<br>λέγων |
| κ. εὐχαριστήσας<br>ἔδωκεν αὐτοῖς λέγων<br>πίετε ἐξ αὐτοῦ πάντες<br>²⁸ τοῦτο γάρ ἐστιν<br>τ. αἷμά μου<br>τ. διαθήκης<br>τ. περὶ πολλῶν ἐκχυννόμενον<br>εἰς ἄφεσιν ἁμαρτιῶν | τοῦτό ἐστι<br>τ. αἷμά μου | τοῦτο τ. ποτήριον<br>ἡ καινὴ διαθήκη<br>ἐν τ. αἵματί μου<br>τ. ὑπὲρ ὑμῶν ἐκχυννόμενον | τοῦτο τ. ποτήριον<br>ἡ καινὴ διαθήκη ἐστὶν<br>ἐν τῷ ἐμῷ αἵματι<br><br>τοῦτο ποιεῖτε<br>ὁσάκις ἐὰν πίνητε<br>εἰς τ. ἐμὴν ἀνάμνησιν |

TABLE XII

| Matt. 26.39 (Justin Dial. 99 2) | Justin Dial. 103.8 | Lk. 22.44,42 |
|---|---|---|
| | [γέγραπται] ὅτι | |
| | | ⁴⁴ [κ. γενόμενος ἐν ἀγωνίᾳ ἐκτενέστερον προσηύχετο κ. ἐγένετο |
| | ἱδρὼς ὡσεὶ θρόμβοι κατεχεῖτο | ὁ ἱδρὼς αὐτοῦ ὡσεὶ θρόμβοι αἵματος καταβαίνοντες ἐπὶ τ. γῆν] |
| προσευχόμενος κ. λέγων πάτερ [μου] εἰ δυνατόν ἐστιν παρελθάτω ἀπ᾽ ἐμοῦ τ. ποτήριον τοῦτο | αὐτοῦ εὐχομένου κ. λέγοντος παρελθέτω εἰ δυνατόν τ. ποτήριον τοῦτο | ⁴¹ προσηύχετο ⁴² λέγων πάτερ εἰ βούλει παρένεγκε τοῦτο τ. ποτήριον ἀπ᾽ ἐμοῦ |
| cf. Justin Dial. 99.2: πάτερ εἰ δυνατόν ἐστι παρελθέτω τ. ποτήριον τοῦτο ἀπ᾽ ἐμοῦ | | |

TABLE XIII

| Matt. 16.21 | Justin Dialogue 51.2 | Justin Dial. 76.7 | Justin Dial. 100.3 | Lk. 24.7 | Lk. 9.22 (cf.Mk.8:31) |
|---|---|---|---|---|---|
| ὅτι δεῖ αὐτὸν εἰς Ἱεροσόλυμα ἀπελθεῖν | ὅτι δεῖ αὐτὸν | δεῖ τ.υἱὸν τ.ἀνθρώπου | δεῖ τ.υἱὸν τ.ἀνθρώπου | τ.υἱὸν τ.ἀνθρώπου ὅτι δεῖ | ὅτι δεῖ τ.υἱὸν τ.ἀνθρώπου |
| [cf.17.22] | | | | παραδοθῆναι εἰς χεῖρας ἀνθρώπων ἁμαρτωλῶν | [cf.9.44] |
| κ.πολλὰ παθεῖν | πολλὰ παθεῖν | πολλὰ παθεῖν κ.ἀποδοκιμασθῆναι ὑπὸ | πολλὰ παθεῖν κ.ἀποδοκιμασθῆναι ὑπὸ | | πολλὰ παθεῖν κ.ἀποδοκιμασθῆναι |
| ἀπὸ τ.πρεσβυτέρων κ. ἀρχιερέων | ἀπὸ | | | | ἀπὸ τ.πρεσβυτέρων κ. ἀρχιερέων |
| κ. γραμματέων | τ. γραμματέων κ. φαρισαίων | τ. γραμματέων κ. φαρισαίων | τ. φαρισαίων κ. γραμματέων | | κ. γραμματέων |
| κ. ἀποκτανθῆναι | κ. σταυρωθῆναι | κ. σταυρωθῆναι | κ. σταυρωθῆναι | κ. σταυρωθῆναι | κ. ἀποκτανθῆναι |
| κ.τ.τρίτη ἡμέρα ἐγερθῆναι | κ.τ.τρίτη ἡμέρα ἀναστῆναι.... | κ.τ.τρίτη ἡμέρα ἀναστῆναι | κ.τ.τρίτη ἡμέρα ἀναστῆναι | κ.τ.τρίτη ἡμέρα ἀναστῆναι | κ.τ.τρίτη ἡμέρα ἐγερθῆναι |

# CHAPTER TWO

# THE STRUCTURE OF ACTS AND ITS THEOLOGY

HISTORIANS DO not need to hold definite beliefs in order to do their work, but, when they do believe, their writings inevitably betray that belief. The first clues to a historian's faith are provided by the point at which he chooses to begin his history and the point at which he ends. When Gibbon began his *Decline and Fall of the Roman Empire* with the Antonines in the second century, he revealed his belief that civilizations start to decline when they enjoy an enervating peace in which the "manly spirit of freedom" is dissipated. Or, to take a more recent example, when Tawney ended his *Religion and the Rise of Capitalism* with the state of affairs at the beginning of the eighteenth century, we are left in no doubt of his belief that religion had reached its lowest point when it did nothing but encourage capitalism.

The theology of the author of Acts is strikingly defined by his beginning and his ending. The beginning has added weight because it is also the middle of the complete work, Luke-Acts, but we cannot interpret the significance of the beginning until we know for certain whether the end we have is really the end.

A long line of commentators has found the present ending unsatisfactory because it does not tell us what happened to Paul. They have supposed that Luke had either intended to write a third volume which he never began, or had written a third volume which has disappeared without a trace. The third volume would have chronicled Paul's later journeys, his last trial, and his martyrdom. This is a hypothesis for which there is no evidence apart from Luke-Acts itself, and it is impossible to entertain such a hypothesis unless the existing evidence is otherwise inexplicable. This chapter, and indeed the whole book, is an attempt to show that Acts and its companion Gospel display a clear and coherent pattern and completely serve the purpose of the artist and theologian who wrote them. There is no need to suppose that Luke had not finished his work.

Before we discuss the significance of the end of Acts we must dispose of another attempt to rob it of any particular meaning. In his later writings, Harnack revived the theory that the end of Acts represented the limits of Luke's historical information; he could write no more because he knew no more.[1] This hypothesis fails on two grounds. First, Luke's Gospel was written after the fall of Jerusalem when it is most unlikely that the martyrdom of Paul was unknown. Clement, writing in A.D. 95, knew of it,[2] and there is no reason to suppose that it would be unknown throughout the whole Church, much less unknown to a writer who made St Paul his hero. Second, Acts itself unmistakably indicates that Paul would die in Rome.

Both these grounds have been challenged. The first is challenged by the argument that Luke's Gospel does not, as has long been supposed, refer to the fall of Jerusalem and that there is, therefore, no remaining reason for holding that it was written after A.D. 70; an attempt has already been made to refute it.[3]

It has also been denied that Acts says that Paul would be martyred in Rome. Harnack[4] has argued that the foreboding of death expressed by Paul in his farewell address to the Ephesian elders when he said that they would never see him

[1] *The Date of the Acts and the Synoptic Gospels* (Eng. tr., London, 1911), 93–9.

[2] 1 Clem. 5.7; cf. Conzelmann in Dibelius, *Die Pastoralbriefe* (3rd ed., Tübingen, 1955), 3.

[3] Pages 1–3, above.

[4] *The Acts of the Apostles* (Eng. tr., London, 1909), 293f; *The Date of the Acts* (Eng. tr., London, 1911), 103.

again (20.25,38) was proved wrong by his release from imprisonment in Rome and his new journey to the East. It is no longer possible to hold that Paul wrote the Pastoral Epistles as they stand,[1] and they alone require a release and second imprisonment. The Pastorals themselves mention only one imprisonment, and the need to call this the second springs from an attempt to harmonize the personal references in 2 Tim. 4.9–21 with those in the other letters ascribed to Paul.[2] The foreboding of death in Acts 20, which the author is at pains to underline, would be clearly understood by contemporary readers of Luke's work to have been fulfilled in Paul's martyrdom at Rome.[3]

The fact that Luke made Acts end with Paul's freedom to preach while imprisoned in Rome now appears even more significant. He has put the prophecy of martyrdom as far back as chapter 20 so that it will overshadow the rest of the story, but chooses to conclude not with the martyrdom itself but with the third rejection of the Jews and a period of unhindered preaching to the Gentiles. Paul dominates the bulk of Acts and his death is of great significance, and yet it is less important to portray this death than it is to say that he has arrived and preached in Rome. The end of the history is a place.[4]

We shall not fully understand the significance of Luke's geographical end to Acts unless we take account of the parallel

---

[1] P. N. Harrison, *The Problem of the Pastoral Epistles* (Oxford, 1921).

[2] Conzelmann in Dibelius, op. cit., 3 and 95. 1 Clem. 5.5–7 probably does not imply a visit to Spain and the Muratorian fragment is a speculation based on Rom. 15.24,28; Harrison, ibid., 107f. Ramsay and Lake's attempts to prove that the last verse of Acts implies a release from prison are unconvincing; *Beginnings*, v.319–38; E. Haenchen, *Die Apostelgeschichte* (Meyer Kommentar, 10th ed., Göttingen, 1956), 657f, n 1.

[3] M. Dibelius, *Studies in the Acts of the Apostles* (1951, Eng. tr., London, 1956), 158 and n 1.

[4] *Beginnings*, iv.350. The significance of the geographical data in Luke-Acts has been stressed by R. H. Lightfoot, *History and Interpretation in the Gospels* (London, 1935), and *Locality and Doctrine in the Gospels* (London, 1938); H. Conzelmann, *Die Mitte der Zeit, Studien zur Theologie des Lukas* (Tübingen, 1954) Eng. tr., *The Theology of St Luke* (London, 1960); and W. Marxsen, *Der Evangelist Markus, Studien zur Redaktionsgeschichte des Evangeliums* (Göttingen, 1956).

ending to his Gospel.[1] Acts ends in Rome; the Gospel ends in Jerusalem. It was by no means necessary that the Gospel should end at Jerusalem, and we can see from the way Luke edited Mark that this was the result of a conscious choice. In Mark the angel who announces the resurrection says, "Go, tell his disciples and Peter that he goes before you into Galilee. There you will see him as he told you" (16.7; cf. 14.28). Lohmeyer has suggested that these words refer to the Parousia: "When the disciples go to Galilee, they will there see the Lord, that is, they will experience the Parousia."[2] Whether or not this is so, it is sufficient for us to notice that the saying seems to have become the basis for a number of Galilean resurrection appearances (Matt. 28.16,10,7; John 21; The Gospel of Peter, etc.). Luke takes a more drastic way out than that taken by Matthew. He has removed every trace of a future appearance in Galilee by changing Mark's words to read, "Remember how he said to you while he was in Galilee, 'The Son of man must be delivered into the hands of sinful men, etc.'" (24.6f). Galilee, which in Mark is the place of future revelation, has become the place where Jesus predicted his death and resurrection; it has been put firmly at the beginning of the saga so that Jerusalem should be at the end (cf. Acts 10.37).

There is evidence, then, that Luke wishes his readers to pay particular attention to the place where he ends both his Gospel and Acts. He has confined the resurrection appearances to Jerusalem and its environs at the expense of altering the words of the angel at the Tomb, and he has deliberately omitted the story of Paul's trial and martyrdom so that the fact of his free preaching in Rome will stand out. Jerusalem is more important than Rome, not only because it is the end of Luke's Gospel but

---

[1] J. B. Lightfoot, *St Paul's Epistle to the Philippians* (London, 1868), 3 n 2: "A comparison (of Acts 28.30,31) with the closing sentences of the Gospel shows a striking parallelism in the plan of the two narratives; they end alike, as they had begun alike."

[2] Ernst Lohmeyer, *Galiläa und Jerusalem* (Göttingen, 1936), 10–14. C. F. Evans, "'I will go before you into Galilee'", *J.T.S.*, N.S., v (1954), 3–18, suggests that Jesus was referring to the Gentile mission.

also because it is the mid-point of Luke-Acts.[1] Rome is the goal of the work, but Jerusalem is the centre to which the action of the Gospel proceeds and from which each new advance in Acts begins. Jerusalem is the city which killed Jesus, as it had killed the prophets before him (Luke 13.34; Matt. 23.37); his resurrection appearances took place in and around Jerusalem; he ascended into heaven just outside its walls; the disciples were ordered to remain there until they had received the power of the Holy Spirit. Because Jerusalem possesses this central importance in the history of salvation, it would be a travesty to end with a subordinate death at Rome. Although Paul's martyrdom dominates the last section of Acts, it only dominates it because it reflects the death of Jesus. The ending of Acts teaches that, even though Paul came to Rome to die, he brought with him the victorious gospel which had triumphed at Jerusalem. The reader is told in the clearest possible terms consistent with historical verisimilitude that Paul was going to be martyred in Rome, but no account of the event is given. Rome has not destroyed the gospel in killing Paul, because Jerusalem could not destroy Jesus; Jesus' triumph in Jerusalem has guaranteed the triumph of the gospel in Rome.

Jerusalem clearly has tremendous theological significance for Luke, but the same is also true about Rome. His preoccupation with showing that neither Jesus nor Paul was ever judged guilty by a Roman official and his accounts of the conversion of Roman soldiers betray his desire to win over the Roman Empire to the side of Christianity. Just as Jerusalem at the centre of the story is the place where God's promises are fulfilled despite the rejection of Jesus by the Jews, so Rome at the end is the place where the acceptance of the gospel by the Gentiles can be confidently announced (Acts 28.28).

Because Luke has endowed geographical data with theological meaning we are justified in reopening the question

---

[1] This is mathematically as well as symbolically true. Cadbury has estimated that the Gospel of Luke is within 3 per cent of the length of Acts; *The Book of Acts in History* (London, 1955), 138.

whether the geographical movement of the story might not provide the clue to the detailed structure of Acts. If we know the limits of the "chapters" into which the book is divided—if it is divided at all—we should be in a position to isolate the central concern of each part and to understand more clearly the theology of the whole.[1]

Other principles of division have had their vogue. C. H. Turner put forward the suggestion that there were six generalizing summaries which divided Acts into six panels, three for Peter and three for Paul (6.7; 9.31; 12.24; 16.5; 19.20; 28.31).[2] These summaries, however, lack regularity of form[3] and, though they are perhaps the most generalized one can find in Acts, there are a number of other summaries dotted around in a way that suggests that Luke does not intend to divide his narrative by a single trick of style. The summaries play no fixed rôle in the book: 9.31 seems to link two sections rather than to divide them, summarizing the results of the missionary work in preparation for the account of Peter's tour of review; 12.24 marks no more than a stage in the story, a general formula expressing optimism at what has just happened, before the work of Barnabas and Paul is taken up again. Luke's Gospel shows even more clearly the varied functions the summaries are able to perform; in 4.14 and 37, for example, they are put to work to mark off one small but significant section.

The untidiness and incompleteness of some of the panels enclosed by the summaries (in 16.5, as Cadoux notes, "the 'rubric of progress' . . . comes right in the middle of Paul's visit to the various cities he had already evangelized on his first missionary journey"), have led Cadoux and Bacon to argue that the summaries mark chronological divisions (or at least Luke thought that they marked chronological divisions)

[1] Cf. the illuminating division of Matt. into five blocks of narrative and teaching, B. W. Bacon, *Studies in Matthew* (1930).

[2] Hastings, *Dictionary of the Bible*, i.421; *Beginnings*, ii.175-7 and Cadbury's important criticism, ibid. 392-402.

[3] Cf. the standard rubrics in Matt. 7.28; 11.1; 13.53; 19.1; 26.1.

of five years each.[1] But if the sections are not complete and coherent in their subject matter, the dividing lines must be drawn particularly firmly and unmistakably in order to be convincing. If Luke had meant to attach this importance to chronology we should expect much more definite chronological notes than the intermittent and unconnected references to time scattered through Acts (years and months are specified in 11.26; 18.11; 19.8,10; 20.3,31; 24.27; 28.11,30, and days much more often, mostly in the "we"-sections). The summaries are not dated, nor are they attached to dated events. We must conclude that Luke did not intend to divide his work by the summaries. A successful hypothesis about the structure of Acts should both take account of the specific indications Luke chooses to give, and separate the narrative, the illustrative incidents, the speeches, and the summaries into natural groupings; a division by summaries alone does not fulfil these requirements.

Jerusalem and Rome are linked together in Jesus' last charge to his disciples: "You will receive power when the Holy Spirit comes upon you, and you will be my witnesses in Jerusalem, in the whole of Judea and Samaria, and to the end of the earth" (1.8). Many commentators have taken this to be a summary of the contents of Acts,[2] but few have pressed it into service to indicate the divisions of the work. Knowling,[3] taking his cue from J. B. Lightfoot, suggests that the contents may be divided, according to 1.8, into three sections: 2.14—8.1, "in Jerusalem"; 8.2—11.18, "in all Judea and Samaria", and 11.19—28.31, "and to the uttermost part of the earth". With a slight adjustment to make the first part begin with 1.9,

---

[1] C. J. Cadoux, "The Chronological Division of Acts", *J.T.S.*, xix (1917–18), 333–41; the quotation in brackets, 336. B. W. Bacon, "The Chronological Scheme of Acts", *H.T.R.*, xiv (1921), 137–66, emphasizes that the panels marked 5-year periods in Luke's mind, even though he may have been mistaken.

[2] The first, as far as I know, was Mayerhoff (1835), cited by McGiffert, *Beginnings*, ii.366.

[3] *The Acts of the Apostles* in *The Expositor's Greek Testament* ii (London, 1900), 11.

immediately after the introduction,[1] and the second with 8.4, so that Stephen's martyrdom is complete in the preceding verse, Knowling's scheme seems to correspond with Luke's indication in 1.8, and to group the events in a natural way. The second and third divisions both begin a new advance by referring back in similar words to Stephen's martyrdom: οἱ μὲν οὖν διασπαρέντες διῆλθον . . . (8.4; 11.19).

If the scheme so well begun is to provide a complete account of the structure of the book it must be extended to supply at least one, and possibly more than one, division in Knowling's long third section. Menoud,[2] after rightly disposing of the attempt to divide Acts at the end of chapter 12 into The Acts of Peter and The Acts of Paul, argues that the real dividing line comes after 15.35. He relies on two arguments: first, by the time of the Council of Jerusalem all the steps have been made in principle to take the gospel to the end of the earth— geographically the gospel has been taken beyond Jerusalem, Judea, and Samaria to Asia Minor, and theologically the Gentiles are admitted on an equal footing into the Church— and second, after the Council Paul embarks on a long journey which bears a new character, and he is now raised to the apostolic dignity of "witness". These arguments seem to be strong enough to justify putting a new division after 15.35, but not strong enough to require making it the division which dominates all other divisions. It is true that the Council of Jerusalem marks the last discussion of the validity of the Gentile mission, but it is not the first. It is nothing to say that in principle the whole of the geographical advance has been made with the preaching of the gospel in Asia Minor, for in principle the geographical movement outside Palestine was made by Jesus' prophetic last words to his disciples,[3] and even when Paul comes to Rome the total extent of the movement to the end of the earth is still only in principle accomplished.[4] Paul

---

[1] The introduction does not end with 1.5; Haenchen, 117.

[2] "Le Plan des Actes des Apôtres", *N.T.S.*, i (1954), 44–51.

[3] Paul Wendland, *Die Urchristlichen Literaturformen*, Hdb.z.N.T., I.iii (2nd and 3rd ed., Tübingen, 1912), XII, *Apostelgeschichten*, 317.

[4] Knowling, op. cit., 12.

certainly assumes full control of his missionary enterprise after the Council, but there is no indication that Luke now elevates him to a new status; Paul believes that he has been a "witness" ever since the Lord appeared to him on the Damascus road (22.15; 26.16). Finally, if Paul plays a more important part after the Jerusalem Council, he assumes yet another rôle in the last section of the book, when his journey up to Jerusalem, and from Jerusalem to Rome, is reminiscent of Jesus' journey to his death.[1] We are fully justified in making 15.35 the end of the third division of Acts, but not in regarding it as the only division.

Menoud[2] rightly rejects the old scheme for dividing Paul's missionary journeys into "the first missionary journey" (13–14), "the second missionary journey" (15.36—18.22), and "the third missionary journey" (18.23—21.14 or 16). That scheme not only derives from a missionary practice which had clear ideas about the fixed "headquarters" from which missionaries were sent out, but also ignores the explicit indications of another pattern in Acts itself. It is clear from these that a new stage begins at 19.21.[3] In 19.10 Luke notes that after two years' preaching in Ephesus it could be said that "all those who lived in Asia, Jews and Greeks, had heard the word of the Lord"; the words at the opening of 19.21, "when these things had been completed", refer not just to the events which took place during Paul's stay in Ephesus but to his whole missionary activity in Asia. From the beginning of the section there is a divine compulsion behind every step that is taken. The ambiguous words ἔθετο ὁ Παῦλος ἐν τῷ πνεύματι tell the discerning reader that the Holy Spirit has inspired Paul's resolve,[4] as the word δεῖ, denoting divine necessity, shows: "After I have been there (in Jerusalem), it is necessary for me to see Rome too." We are reminded of the words Ananias heard in 9.16, when the Lord said to him, "I will show him (Paul) how much it is

---

[1] R. B. Rackham, *The Acts of the Apostles* (London, 1901), xlvii.
[2] Op. cit., 48f.
[3] *Beginnings*, iv.243: "This is the real beginning of Paul's last journey to Jerusalem."      [4] Ibid., iv.244.

necessary (δεῖ) that he suffer for my name's sake." Again and again in the next chapters the Spirit tells Paul that he will undergo suffering and eventually stand before Caesar in Rome; Paul tells the Ephesian elders about the Spirit's repeated assurance that this will be so (20.22f, 25, cf. 38); the disciples at Tyre warn him against going to Jerusalem (21.4); Agabus prophesies his arrest in Jerusalem (21.10–14), and the Lord confirms his purpose to send Paul to Rome by appearing to him when he is arrested in Jerusalem (23.11: δεῖ), and again during the great storm on his way to the capital (27.24).

There is an unmistakable unity in this last section. The key to its significance is to be found in the way Paul replies to Agabus in 21.13: "Why do you weep and break my heart? I am ready not only to be bound but to die in Jerusalem for the sake of the name of the Lord Jesus." At first sight we are surprised that he should think it likely that he would die in Jerusalem when he has already stated, "It is necessary for me to see Rome" (19.21), but plainly what he means to indicate is that he is willing to follow the pattern of Christ's suffering, who was also delivered up by the Jews into the hands of the Gentiles (21.11).[1] The repeated predictions of his suffering correspond to Jesus' own predictions as he too travelled up to Jerusalem. Paul, however, is rescued from death again and again (21.31–6; 23.12–24; 25.2ff; 27.24,42f; 28.3ff) so that he will at last arrive safely in Rome. There, as Luke clearly tells us, he is martyred, but that is no climax: the climax is his arrival and his unrestricted preaching at the centre of the Empire. The sufferings by which this goal is achieved are literally Christ-like, but if Luke had gone on to recount how Paul died he would have obscured the gospel message: the spiritual conquest of the Empire depended on Jesus' death and resurrection in Jerusalem, not on Paul's death in Rome. While it is true that Acts parallels the third Gospel, and in particular the final sections of each correspond, the more important thing to see is that both books hinge on what happened in Jerusalem.

---

[1] Overbeck; see Haenchen, op. cit., 542.

Jerusalem is the centre of Luke-Acts, the centre of the history of salvation.[1]

Before we can confidently draw any further conclusions from the suggested division of Acts into five sections, we must see whether these divisions correspond to anything in Luke; it is not necessary that the Gospel and Acts should be constructed in exactly the same way but, if the Gospel appears to be built on entirely different principles from those which we have suggested for Acts, the hypothesis would lose a great deal of its force.

Commentators usually put divisions in Luke's Gospel at three places: the first either just before or just after Jesus' temptations (4.1 or 4.14), the second when he sets his face to go to Jerusalem (9.51), and the third as he prepares for his triumphant entry into the city (19.28). The fact that the long central section, 9.51 to 19.28, is cast in the form of a journey suggests that geographical factors may be as important for the division of the Gospel as they are for Acts.[2] The usual divisions can be defined geographically. After the Temptations Jesus returns to Galilee (4.14) and seems to have used Galilee as his base for preaching throughout all Judea (4.44; 7.17) before withdrawing to Bethsaida in the north of Galilee (9.10) to prepare his disciples for his journey. Apart from an initial incursion into Samaria (9.51–6), the journey itself seems to have taken place mainly in Galilee, or more vaguely "between Samaria and Galilee" (17.11); the only fixed point is the goal, Jerusalem (9.51; 13.22,33f; 17.11; 18.31; 19.11). The factor which defines the shape of the narrative in this long journey section is not the towns through which the travellers pass—none is mentioned by name until they approach Jericho (18.35)—but the way Jesus explains to his disciples his own fate, and the way he prepares them for their discipleship. "Jesus' consciousness that he must suffer is expressed in the form of a journey" (Conzelmann).[3]

---

[1] Cf. Conzelmann, *Die Mitte der Zeit* (Tübingen, 1954), 8f, *The Theology of St Luke* (London, 1960), 16f.

[2] R. H. Lightfoot; H. Conzelmann.     [3] Op. cit., 53, Eng. tr., 65.

If this is so, there is good reason for believing that Luke has grouped the teaching contained in the travel narrative into two sections. The division occurs at 14.1. Just before this new section, Jesus defines again his purpose to go to Jerusalem, under pressure of the warning conveyed by the Pharisees that Herod is trying to kill him. Luke has marked the beginning of the journey by stating Jesus' firm intention to go to Jerusalem, but his purpose is not yet fully defined (9.51); at the end of chapter 13 the intention is repeated, and this time it is made clear by the lament over Jerusalem that the city will kill him as it killed the prophets before him.

It would be out of place to attempt to justify the new division in detail, but there are at least three indications that this is the way Luke meant to divide his Gospel.

First, Jesus' answer to the Pharisees who warn him of the danger from Herod suggests that the journey should be divided into two parts: "See, I cast out demons and perform healings to-day and to-morrow, and on the third day I will reach my goal. But it is necessary for me to journey to-day and to-morrow and the next day, because it is not God's will (ἐνδέχεται) that a prophet should perish outside Jerusalem" (13.32f). "The third day I will reach my goal" obviously refers to the last period of his life when he enters Jerusalem, and it is possible that "to-day" and "to-morrow" represent stages in the journey to his destination.

Second, the content of the teaching in the second part of the journey seems to be developed a stage further than it was in the first half. The clue to the difference may be found in the contrast between the two similar parables of the friend at midnight and the importunate widow. Each is constructed according to the same pattern and each teaches the same lesson, but one occurs in the first half of the journey (11.5–8) and the other in the second half (18.1–8). The significant difference is that the first parable concerns the need for bread and the second the need for help in oppression. This distinction seems to be typical of the difference in emphasis in each part: the first part is full of teaching about the nature of discipleship, its duties, hardships, and rewards, while in the second part the opposition to Jesus comes out into the open and the disciples are taught how they must behave under persecution.

Third, the three occasions on which Jesus dines with Pharisees correspond to the three central sections of the Gospel. The first is taken over from Mark (Mark 14.3–9; Luke 7.36–50), but Luke has radically altered its place in the narrative; the second (Luke 11.37ff) contains the Woes from Q, but their setting during a meal with a Pharisee is found in Luke alone; the opening of the third meal (Luke 14.1ff) seems to be a Lucan repetition of an earlier incident (Luke 6.6–11 and par.), an indication that Luke is responsible for the setting here as well. The first meal occurs in the section where Jesus gathers his disciples together, the second in the first part of the journey, and the third in the second part of the journey and each meal shows a development in the relationship between Jesus and the Pharisees of increasing antagonism, corresponding to the stages on the spiritual journey to Jerusalem.

It is possible, then, to justify a five-fold division of the Gospel: (1) 1.5 to 3.38, Jesus comes to fulfil all the O.T. expectations; (2) 4.1 to 9.50, he preaches in the whole of Judea and Galilee and gathers his disciples; (3) 9.51 to 13.35, he begins his journey to Jerusalem and teaches the nature of discipleship; (4) 14.1 to 19.27, he concludes his journey to Jerusalem and prepares his disciples for the Passion; (5) 19.28 to 24.53, he reigns in Jerusalem by dying and rising again.

Each of the parts is governed by some sort of geographical factor, and always the geographical movement has significance for the history of salvation. The city which appears at every turn of the story is the holy city of Jerusalem, and it is important to note that at each of the breaks between Luke's sections there stands a definitive reference to Jerusalem. At the first Jesus, after his baptism in the Jordan, is led into the desert by the Spirit to be tempted and his last temptation takes place in Jerusalem; his mission is defined near Jerusalem before he returns to Galilee to begin his ministry (4.14). At the second break he steadfastly sets his face to go to Jerusalem (9.51); at the third he renews his purpose to die in Jerusalem and laments over the rebellious city (13.31–5); at the fourth he enters it to die, having warned his disciples that Jerusalem cannot be the scene of the Kingdom's coming until it has been the scene of his death (19.11ff).

The corresponding five-fold division of Acts is this: (1) 1.9 to 8.3; (2) 8.4 to 11.18; (3) 11.19 to 15.35; (4) 15.36 to 19.20; (5) 19.21 to 28.31.

Jerusalem is equally important for this set of divisions. Stephen's martyrdom is the signal to take the gospel from Jerusalem to Judea and Samaria, and to Antioch and beyond, providing both the first and the second break in the story (8.4 and 11.19). At the beginning of each of these second and third sections the Jerusalem Church specifically approves and watches over the new missionary efforts, by sending Peter and John to Samaria (8.14–25) and by sending Barnabas to Antioch (11.22ff). The second section ends with Peter reporting back to Jerusalem after he has baptized Cornelius, and receiving the blessing of the Jerusalem Church on his work (11.18). The break between the third and fourth sections is marked by the important Jerusalem Council in which, significantly, James the leader of the Jerusalem Church and not Peter the first of the Apostles takes the principal part. The final section begins with Paul making his fateful decision to return to Jerusalem and to go from there to Rome.

In the whole of Luke-Acts Jerusalem controls the history. It is at the same time the city which God redeems (Luke 2.38) and the city where he is rejected. It becomes the centre of the mission to the Gentiles, but it rejects the gospel for itself. Jerusalem is both the Heavenly City and the Earthly City. The story ends at Rome because Jerusalem has rejected her saviour, but Rome will be the centre of the Church, and Jerusalem will be in subjection, only "until the times of the Gentiles are fulfilled" (Luke 21.24).

The most cogent objection to seeing the structure of Acts in a geographical framework is made by Overbeck. "The view that Acts is intended to describe the passage of the Gospel from Jerusalem to Rome . . . collapses at once before the fact that in 28.15 Acts presupposes the existence of a Christian community in Rome, without having announced its origin. We are not told how the Gospel came to Rome, but how Paul came to Rome."[1]

This objection cannot be avoided by saying that here is another example of the contradiction between Luke's scheme and his sources, his scheme demanding that Paul be the first missionary in Rome, though his sources have stated that there was already a Christian congregation in the city.[2] We are told too often about the Christians already established in the place when Paul first arrives for this argument to succeed. The existence of Christians in Ephesus seems to be assumed, although they are still part of the Synagogue (18.19ff,26; Priscilla and Aquila) and there are "brethren" at Puteoli to greet Paul on his way to Rome (28.13f).[3] In the same way Peter finds Christians already in Lydda and Joppa (9.32,36), and perhaps we should also note that Jesus is greeted by a "crowd of disciples" when he enters Jerusalem, though he has conducted no mission in the city (Luke 19.37). Luke does not seem to be primarily interested in how the gospel was first planted in the cities of the Empire.

Another answer is to turn the objection back on those who make it by admitting that Luke emphasizes the arrival of Paul at Rome, and asserting that, if this is not the first occasion, it is the definitive occasion on which the gospel is preached in the capital. Menoud says: "The 'chosen vessel' is not the first to preach the gospel in the city of the Caesars. But in the eyes of Luke it is Paul who, coming from Jerusalem in the fellowship of the Apostles, and invested by Christ himself with the status of witness, is the missionary truly authorized in every respect,

[1] F. Overbeck, *Introduction to De Wette's Commentary on Acts* (4th ed., 1870), in the English translation of Zeller, *The Contents and Origin of the Acts of the Apostles, Critically Investigated* (London, 1875), 16; cf. Cadoux, op. cit., 334f.

[2] Cadoux, op. cit., 335.

[3] Haenchen, op. cit., 663.

the one qualified to carry out Christ's command to proclaim the gospel to the world."[1]

This approach seems to be the right one, but it goes too far. Granted that Paul is the "hero" of Acts, we may doubt whether the mere fact of his arrival in Rome would be sufficient to mark the preliminary completion of Jesus' command in 1.8. The full significance of the geographical stages according to which Acts is constructed cannot be contained in a simple statement that Paul, the foremost missionary, has arrived at his goal, since the geographical forward-movement depends on many others besides Paul, and begins before his conversion. But if Acts is not the story of how the good news was brought from Jerusalem to Rome, and not simply the story of how Paul, as Christ's chief evangelist, reached Rome, what is it?

In Ephesus, the other main city where Paul finds Christians when he arrives, we discover a clue to the decisive nature of Paul's work in Rome. The Christians still seem to have been members of the synagogue, for it was in the synagogue that Priscilla and Aquila heard Apollos teaching a defective doctrine about Jesus (18.24–8), and Paul had already been treated well by the same synagogue a little earlier (18.19–21). When Paul returned to Ephesus he also had to deal with disciples who only knew John's baptism, and he spent three months in the synagogue reasoning and trying to persuade the Jews to become Christians (19.8). Only when they proved adamant and began counter-propaganda did Paul feel obliged to separate off the disciples and find another preaching-place (19.9). When two years of this separatist preaching had been completed Luke can say that "all who live in Asia, Jews and Greeks, had heard the word of the Lord" (19.10). It seems that Paul's particular work, in Ephesus at least, had not consisted in simply preaching in order to make Christians: Christians there were already; what Paul's preaching to the Jews accomplished was the

---

[1] Op. cit., 50; cf. Knowling, op. cit., 13; "The Gospel had come to Rome already, but those who accepted it were only a sect everywhere spoken against; now its foremost representative gains it a hearing from the Gentiles, and that too without interruption or prohibition."

ejection of the Christians from the synagogue and the founding
of a separate church. A similar scene had been enacted as a
result of Paul's preaching in Pisidian Antioch (13.46) and in
Corinth (18.6), and was to occur again in Rome (28.28).[1] It is
inadequate to say that the theme of Acts is the spread of the
gospel from Jerusalem to Rome, because the gospel has run
ahead of Paul from Jerusalem to Rome. The decisive effect of
his preaching is the establishment of the Church as an institu-
tion separate from Judaism. Luke's thesis is that the gospel is
free to travel to the ends of the earth only when it is free from
the false form which the Jewish religion has taken. Paul is the
one figure in the early Church who saw the issue clearly, and
that is why Luke makes Paul the central figure in the latter
part of Acts. Paul does not attack the Jews—far from it—but
when he goes to them and states the issues they eventually turn
on him and, as God has fore-ordained, reject the gospel.
Right up to the last journey to Jerusalem Paul has regarded
the Church as still essentially part of the Jewish nation. The
only reference to the collection he brought up to Jerusalem
makes this clear: "Now, after some years I came bringing relief
to my nation . . ." not, let it be noted, specifically to the
Church which can be distinguished from the nation (24.17).
At his trials and examinations he emphasizes that he has
remained a faithful Jew: "I have not sinned in any respect
against the Law of the Jews, against the Temple or against
Caesar" (25.8; cf. 23.6). Yet still the Jews try to kill him and
refuse to accept the gospel, so that, with a note of finality, he
is at length forced to declare, "Let it be known to you that this,
the salvation of God, has been sent to the Gentiles. They will
hear" (28.28). The process which first became obvious when
Stephen was martyred has come to its ordained conclusion.
While the gospel spread from Jerusalem in ever-widening
circles until it reached Rome, another process was at work.
The gospel was breaking out of its entanglement with organized Judaism and becoming free to be the universal religion.
Jerusalem is left behind and Rome is entered.

[1] Dibelius, op. cit. (Eng. tr.), 149f.

# CHAPTER THREE

# THE ATTITUDE TO THE JEWS

IT WAS suggested in the previous chapter that the movement of the story from Jerusalem to Rome had more than a matter-of-fact significance. Luke means to show that the Church came of age when it finally left Jerusalem behind. In this chapter we shall explore more thoroughly that part of Luke's theology of history which concerns the Jews who have not repented, and try, by referring to historical parallels, to place this theology in the development of Christian thought.

The best starting point for the exploration is Stephen's speech. One of the chief difficulties in understanding Luke's own theology is that one can never be sure that the sentiments he attributed to any of his characters are precisely what he himself believed; he may either have had good historical information about what they said on a particular occasion, or he may have thought that he knew well enough what they would have said without himself agreeing with it all. The best way of discovering his own point of view is by noting, as we have tried to do in the previous chapter, what he chooses to tell and what he omits, where he begins and where he ends. Luke believed that the history of the apostolic period displayed the working of God as directly as the history of Jesus' life had done, and he felt justified in making his second volume balance and complete the first. His theology must be looked for primarily in the movement of his history. If the speeches differ from one another in theological emphasis, we must not expect to hear Luke's voice in one as against the other, but we should look for his theology in the dramatic contribution each of them makes to the progress of the story. The relationship of the speeches to one another in their similarities and differences is more important for our purpose than the contents of each of them taken by itself.

Stephen's speech provides a good place to begin, for two reasons. First, it occurs at the first great crisis of Acts. The martyrdom of Stephen forms the conclusion of the first of the five sections into which it seems that Luke divided his work. It is the last event which takes place while the action is confined to Jerusalem, and the persecution which follows is specifically pointed out as marking the beginning of the next two stages in the story, set first in Samaria, Judea, and Galilee (8.4—11.18) and then in southern Asia Minor (11.19—15.35). Further, it is the event which first involves Saul of Tarsus in Christian history. By the way in which so much of significance is attached to one event we may suspect that Luke is schematizing the history and attributing to one cause what probably should be attributed to many. It would be wrong to call this falsification; rather he is illustrating with one concrete example the historical truth that the indifference and hostility of the Jews led to the spread of the gospel beyond Palestine. But his art betrays his theology.

Second, we begin with Stephen's speech because it is so very different in form and contents from any other speech in Acts. Its theology seems to be unparalleled, and yet Luke thought it sufficiently important to devote more space to it than to any other speech. The source may have been lengthy, but he was free to shorten or omit as he pleased; if his sources did contain reports of speeches, he must have omitted some and shortened others (cf. the summary in one verse of what Paul preached to Felix in 24.25), so that we are obliged to ask what significance Stephen's speech had for Luke. We shall be nearer the answer if we can understand the part played by the speech in the development of Acts as a whole.

The first question, however, concerns the point of the speech at the trial. The commentary on Stephen's speech in *The Beginnings of Christianity* asserts uncompromisingly that "this is

not a rebuttal of the charges brought against him".[1] In a sense
this is true—Stephen does not defend himself by disposing of
the indictments like a man who wants to save his life—but it is
false if it suggests that there is not a complete correspondence
between the charges and the defence.[2]

The evidence shows that Luke took great care over his report
of the formulation of the charge concerning the Temple.
Previously, in his account of Jesus' trial, he has deliberately
omitted the Marcan report of how the false witnesses had
testified to hearing Jesus say, "I shall destroy this Temple
made with hands, and in three days I shall build another not
made with hands" (Mark 14.58). He puts the first part of this
report into the mouths of the false witnesses at Stephen's trial:
"For we have heard him saying that this Jesus, the Nazarene,
will destroy this place . . ." (Acts 6.14),[3] and the Marcan word
χειροποίητος appears later, in Stephen's speech (Acts 7.48).
Luke knew that Stephen had been charged with some sort of
subversion, and he has supplied the charge by transposing part
of Jesus' trial scene as recorded in Mark. Since Luke formulated
the charge, he must have believed that the speech answered it.

Marcel Simon draws entirely different conclusions from this
evidence.[4] He believes that the charge was made against
Stephen because he "had actually taken up a position utterly
hostile to the Temple", and that Luke, who disagreed with
Stephen, did his best to minimize the matter. For that reason
he omitted the charge from Jesus' trial; "he may have thought

---

[1] *Beginnings*, iv.69; cf. Wendland, *Hdb.z.N.T.*, I.iii (Tübingen, 1912),
265; F. J. Foakes Jackson, *J.B.L.*, 1930, 283–6; Bo Reicke, *Glaube und
Leben der Urgemeinde* (Zürich, 1957), 133, who states that the speech is
primarily a sermon and only "indirectly intended as a speech in defence".

[2] B. S. Easton, "A Note on Stephen's Speech" at the end of "The
Purpose of Acts" in *Early Christianity* (London, 1955), 115–18.

[3] The substitution in Acts 6.14 of τὸν τόπον τοῦτον for Mark's τὸν ναὸν
τοῦτον does not imply that Luke possessed another source. Luke seems to
reserve the word ναός for the actual sanctuary or shrine (cf. Acts 19.24,27)
and employs the Hellenistic Jewish periphrasis for the Temple, τόπος. See
article in Bauer-Arndt-Gingrich, 830, 1b.

[4] *St Stephen and the Hellenists in the Primitive Church* (The Haskell Lectures,
London, 1958), 24–6.

6

it wiser not to refer to the accusation more than once". The weakness of Simon's argument is that it would have been perfectly easy for Luke to have omitted all reference to what Jesus was supposed to have said; if he was capable of omitting the charge at Jesus' trial, he would have been equally capable of omitting it from Stephen's. Stephen could still have been charged with speaking against the Temple and the Law without Jesus' name being brought in, and Luke could have left his readers to assume that Stephen represented an aberrant form of Christianity.

Why then does Luke remove the charge from the Gospel and raise it again at Stephen's trial? The clue is given by his omission of the second part of Mark's charge, " . . . and in three days I shall build another not made with hands". With these words Mark has transformed a false charge into a true one, if the reader has eyes to see. When Jesus dies the Temple ceases to be God's dwelling place, and at his Resurrection his body becomes the new Temple. The false charge consists only of the first clause, "I shall destroy this Temple . . .", and it seems that Luke was only concerned with a genuinely false charge. Like Jesus and Stephen, Paul also is falsely accused of attacking the Temple (Acts 21.28; 25.8). Luke seems to have taken the opportunity in the space of Stephen's long speech to answer a charge made against Christianity in general.

The other charge levelled at both Stephen and Jesus was that they attacked the Law and wished to change the Mosaic customs (6.11,13,14). Again there is evidence from other parts of Luke-Acts that Luke believed that this was a general charge against Christianity; again it seems likely that he uses Stephen's speech to rebut it. Luke omits the only passage in Mark where Jesus explicitly abrogates the Law of Moses (Mark 10.1–9, the prohibition of divorce),[1] and he repeatedly shows Paul defending himself by word and deed against the accusation that he has broken the Law (Acts 21.17–26; 25.8; 28.17).

The answers to the two charges in the speech are very clear;

---

[1] The prohibition itself appears in Luke 16.19, but the argument against Moses is omitted.

the confusion arises only because there seems to be so much else besides. The answer to the first charge, that Christianity was attacking the Temple, was that the Temple was not God's dwelling place, as the O.T. prophets had already made clear. Jesus was not going to destroy the Temple; if it was destroyed, the implication is, that would be due to the rebelliousness of the Jews who built it and claimed that God lived there. Similarly, not Christianity but Judaism has been disobedient to the Law of Moses, as shown in the rejection of the prophets culminating in the rejection of Jesus. In both cases Stephen turns back the charge on to the Jews, and demonstrates that they, and not the Christians, have disobeyed God and Moses. "The true representatives of the religion of Abraham, Moses and the prophets are not the Jews, ever stubborn and rebellious, but the Christians."[1]

Commentators have attempted to find more in Stephen's speech than this. They have hoped to discover an esoteric theology in the seemingly harmless details of O.T. history. It is true that there are differences between the story as given by Stephen and as recorded in the O.T., but these differences are not significant theologically. They provide one more piece of evidence that Luke is indebted to Hellenistic Jewish sources; most of the discrepancies can be found in Philo and Josephus.[2] The history is not told in order to illustrate the general lesson that God is not tied to one special Holy Land, for there is no attempt to avoid mentioning God's promise that Abraham's descendants would inherit Palestine;[3] there is not enough evidence to prove that Luke held some rudimentary version of a theory of biblical "couples", Moses-Aaron, David-Solomon;[4] nor is Stephen represented as a typologist except in so far as he takes Moses' words about "a prophet like me" to refer to Jesus, and regards the way the Jews treated Jesus as typical.[5] As Dibelius has emphasized, the very neutrality of the O.T.

[1] Loisy, Les Actes des Apôtres (Paris, 1920), 320.
[2] H. J. Cadbury, The Book of Acts in History (London, 1955), 102–4.
[3] Bo Reicke, op. cit., 134 and passim.
[4] Marcel Simon, op. cit., 57.
[5] R. P. C. Hanson, Theology, 50 (1947), 142–5.

narrative is part of Luke's counter to the charges made against Stephen and against Christianity. The first open attack on the Jews is made by a pious Hellenistic Jew, who uses an orthodox O.T. narrative to do it.[1]

How do the answers to the two charges compare with the answers given in the rest of Acts and in Luke's Gospel? Is Stephen's speech almost completely aberrant, and does it "conflict with the basic attitude of Acts"?[2]

At first sight Stephen's attitude to the Temple seems to be shared by no one else in Luke-Acts. Jesus is presented at the Temple according to the Law governing the first-born male; he goes up with his parents when he is twelve; he cleanses the Temple; and he spends the last period of his ministry teaching day after day in the Temple (19.47—21.38). After the ascension the disciples pray continually in the Temple and teach the people there; Paul, according to one account of his conversion, received his commission to go to the Gentiles while he was praying in the Temple (Acts 22.17); and on his last visit to Jerusalem he punctiliously fulfils Temple ceremonial and sponsors four others who had taken a vow (21.23ff). Paul speaks not only for himself but for the whole Christian community when he denies the ridiculous charge that he had tried to profane the Temple (24.6,17–19) and says, "I have committed no offence against either the Law of the Jews, the Temple, or Caesar" (25.8).

On closer examination, however, it appears that Luke is well aware that the Temple is to be destroyed and that the piety centred on the Temple will fail. In the cleansing of the Temple he removes the last part of the quotation from Isa. 56.7 on Jesus' lips: "My house will be a house of prayer" (Luke 19.46), not "My house will be called a house of prayer

---

[1] *Aufsätze* (Göttingen, 1951), 143–6; Eng. tr., *Studies* (London, 1956), 166–9. Haenchen, op. cit., 246ff., follows Dibelius in arguing that Luke has employed a source. Luke's only additions to the source are the polemic sentences at the end of the sections on Moses and Solomon.

[2] Marcel Simon, op. cit., 43; and "Saint Stephen and the Jerusalem Temple", *J.E.H.*, ii (1951), 127.

for all nations" (Mark 11.17).[1] The destruction of the Temple has made it no longer possible to regard it as the place where Gentiles will come to pray. Nor is it without significance that Paul is arrested and accused of profaning the Temple at the very moment when he is paying particular attention to its purificatory requirements. Just as God had told him to go to the Gentiles as he was praying in the Temple, so he is arrested and begins his fateful journey to Rome when he is about to complete the days of purification. It seems that God himself is driving Christians out of the Temple, and showing that they cannot confine themselves to its limitations.

So Luke is able to do justice to the faithfulness of the primitive Church to its Jewish background, while showing at the same time that God is at work in its history to force it out into the Gentile world. Luke uses Stephen's prophetic words before he dies to proclaim God's ancient judgement on the Temple, which the Church only learnt for itself by bitter, but providential, experience.

Stephen's views on the Law are not so strikingly different from those expressed by other Christians in Acts.[2] He is certainly not saying that the Law is an enemy from whom Christians have been freed, as Paul says in his Epistles. He simply states that the Jews themselves have not kept the Law, and implies that they, not he, have attacked it in attacking the prophets and the Messiah. There is no suggestion in the speech that the Jewish charge of antinomianism is justified. It is true that Peter is aware that all Jews, Christian and non-Christian, find it impossible to keep the Law perfectly, and both he and Paul know that keeping the Law is not sufficient for salvation (15.10f; 13.38f), but they never say that Jews are now free to disregard Moses. Paul readily accepts James's plan for publicly demonstrating that he has never tried to turn the Jews of the

---

[1] The same omission is made by Matt. (21.13), probably for the same reason; Kilpatrick, *The Origins of the Gospel according to St Matthew* (Oxford, 1946), 118.

[2] For the whole subject of the Lucan attitude to the Law see the excellent discussion in Leonhard Goppelt, *Christentum und Judentum im ersten und zweiten Jahrhundert* (Gütersloh, 1954), 231–3.

Dispersion away from that allegiance (21.20–6). On one point God himself has had to intervene to make it possible for Jewish Christians to associate with Gentiles in order to preach the gospel to them. He sent to Peter a vision of unclean beasts and commanded him to eat them. This same precedent is invoked in chapter 15 to justify not asking Gentile Christians to be circumcised and fulfil all the special Mosaic practices, but the Jerusalem decree does ask them to accept some limitations: to refrain from eating food offered to idols, strangled animals and blood, and from indulging in fornication (15.20,29; 21.25).[1] The argument for specifying these restrictions seems to be that Mosaic morality is not a purely Palestinian thing, but is well known throughout the Gentile world because of the existence of synagogues in every city.[2] Some parts of the Law of Moses are particularly Jewish, but one may distinguish between those customs (ἔθη) and the universal morality which it contains. All Christians should accept Moses as their moral guide.[3] It seems then that Stephen's defence of Christianity, with its reverence for the Law "received at the command of angels", is not untypical of the attitude to the Law in the rest of Luke-Acts.

His attack on the Jews for themselves not keeping the Law is no fiercer than Paul's when he rebukes the High Priest Ananias for ordering him to be struck on the mouth. "God is

---

[1] The reading of Codex Vaticanus should be accepted; the omission of καὶ τῆς πορνείας by p[45] at 15.20 is an omission of the unlike term; the Western reading is an attempt to make the Decree into a purely moral requirement; see C. S. C. Williams, *Alterations to the Text of the Synoptic Gospels and Acts* (Oxford, 1951), 72–5. Hans Waitz, "Das Problem des sog. Apostel-dekrets, usw.", *Z.K.G.*, Dritte Folge vi (1936), 227–63 at 227–31, suggests that it is an application of the Levitical requirements for "the stranger within the gate" to the relations between Jewish and Gentile Christians. This interpretation was anticipated by A. Ritschl, *Theologische Jahrbücher* vi (1847), 301.

[2] This seems to be the meaning of that difficult verse, 15.21. See Haenchen op. cit., 396f; and Chapter Four, below.

[3] Goppelt, op. cit., 232f; "Perhaps Luke is trying to help the Church to understand what is still applicable to their moral behaviour when he alone among N.T. writers distinguishes the ceremonial Law in the νόμος by a special term, the ἔθη of Moses".

going to strike you, you white-washed wall. You sit there judging me by the Law and do you break the Law (παρανομῶν) by ordering me to be struck?'' (23.3).

On both the points of Stephen's speech we must conclude that his defence fits perfectly the theology of the rest of Acts. Stephen's manner of speaking is quite different from that adopted by Peter and Paul and James, or any other spokesmen for Christianity; he comes out with propositions which could never be attributed to them, and he leaves unsaid things which they would say, but he makes his special contribution to the total consistent theology of the whole book. This theology is not a propositional theology, but a theology of history which has room for certain divergencies and even disagreements, provided they all contribute to showing how God's purpose for the Church is worked out in the end.

We are now in a position to see Stephen's speech as part of the developing pattern of Acts, and to draw some conclusions about Luke's estimation of the place of the Jews in salvation-history.

Stephen's speech is an attack on the Jews rather than a measured defence; both charges are thrown back on to the accusers. The heart of the counter-charge is that the Jews have killed the Messiah, and if we examine all the references to the guilt of the Jews for Jesus' death in Acts we shall see how Luke expounds a single view of the place of the Jews in God's plan by means of the divergent ideas expressed by his historical characters.

Luke is always at pains to emphasize that "Herod and Pontius Pilate, with the Gentiles and the people of Israel" (4.27) each played their part in killing Jesus. It is true that in the account of Jesus' trial he shows that Pilate, in condemning him, was doing it in surrender to the will of the Jews (Luke 23.24f; cf. Mark 15.15), but this does not imply that he believed Pilate guiltless.[1] The factual statements in Acts 2.23 and 3.13

---

[1] Conzelmann's attempt, op. cit., 75–8, Eng. tr., 90–3, to show that Luke in Acts 2.23 is really referring to the Jews and not to the Romans is unconvincing. He argues that there is a tension between the sources, where the

make Pilate's part clear, though this is played down in defer-
ence to the Romans, particularly in Peter's speech before
Cornelius (10.39).[1] Luke's primary theological interest, however, is to show how the Jews rejected each opportunity to
repent of what they had done. In each successive speech that
drama is taken to a new point, and Stephen's speech is the end
of a climax.

In the speech at Pentecost Peter contents himself with a bare
recital of the facts, set in a strong framework of divine inevit-
ability: ". . . him, delivered up in the fixed plan and foreknowledge of God, you nailed up and killed by the hands of lawless
men" (2.23). The Jews he is addressing are clearly told of their
responsibility and are offered repentance, but no special
prominence is given to the matter. The next speech, in chapter
3, is markedly more irenic than the formal statement appropriate to Pentecost. There is no compromise on the need for
repentance—"everyone who does not hear that prophet will
be rooted out from the people" (3.23)—but the guilt of cruci-
fying an innocent man is put down to their ignorance, at the
time, of the true status of him whom "the God of Abraham and
Isaac and Jacob, the God of our fathers has glorified". "And
now, my brothers, I know that you acted in ignorance, like
your rulers" (3.17). Although this appeal leads to the conversion of many of the audience, it is also the cause of the first
arrest. At his appearance before the rulers, elders, and scribes,
Peter is able to stress the exclusive claims of Jesus more
strongly than in the previous speech: "In no one else is there
salvation, for no other name under heaven is given to men
which you must use to be saved" (4.12). After the second
arrest the moment of decision for the Jerusalem rulers has

---

Romans and Jews are blamed alike, and Luke's own view, where only the
Jews are guilty. I agree that Luke has emphasized the guilt of the Jews, but
there is no evidence that he believes it is an exclusive guilt.

[1] Luke is anxious to demonstrate that Pilate believed Jesus innocent
(Luke 23.4; Acts 3.13; 13.28), and this is part of his whole case that
Christianity is a law-abiding religion, but the question here is somewhat
different: it is whether Pilate himself was guilty, rather than whether he
judged Jesus guilty.

drawn another stage nearer, as has the moment when the young Church must decide between loyalty to the religious leaders of its own people and loyalty to God. "One must obey God rather than men ... to the obedient God has given the Holy Spirit" (5.29,32). Pilate's part in the crucifixion is not mentioned, and the Jews are confronted with their own guilt as simply as possible: "You laid hands on him and hung him on the tree" (5.30).

Jerusalem has been given a full opportunity to repent of what it has done but, despite some measure of success, Stephen's arrest and trial and lynching mark the final failure of the mission to the capital. Stephen's speech is a commentary on the significance of his own death; he announces that there is now no turning back from the fatal course of Jewish history inaugurated when the people first rebelled against Moses. Up to this point in Acts the O.T. has been used to show that the prophets had looked forward to Jesus; now it is employed to prove that the Jews have never accepted the prophets. Their guilt has culminated in the murder of Jesus, and they have again refused to repent. "Which of the prophets did your fathers not persecute? And they killed those who announced beforehand the coming of the Righteous One, whom you have now betrayed and murdered" (7.52).

The martyrdom is, as we have already argued, the end of the climax in the first section of the Book of Acts. The mission to Jerusalem is no longer the concern of the author, though he provides evidence that it still continues (21.20); he means us to understand that God's judgement has finally been pronounced on Jerusalem at the murder of Stephen. Stephen is vindicated and sees a vision of the Son of Man, but the city as a whole has lost its chance, though individual Jews might still repent. The mission now goes to Samaria, Judea, and Galilee (8.4—11.18) and to southern Asia Minor (11.19—15.35). At the beginning of each of these two sections stands a reference to the impetus given by the persecution which followed Stephen's martyrdom, showing that the obduracy of the Jerusalem Jews has only furthered the spread of the gospel.

The next time Jews are addressed is by Paul in the synagogue at Antioch of Pisidia. The question of guilt for Jesus' death is again raised, but in the presence of these Dispersion Jews it is specifically laid at the door of the inhabitants of Jerusalem. He stresses that it is now the turn of the Dispersion to accept the promises of God and escape the consequences of disbelieving what God has done. "For the inhabitants of Jerusalem and their leaders did not recognize him and fulfilled the words of the prophets, which are read every Sabbath, condemning him, and though they unearthed no capital crime they (still) asked Pilate to have him executed. . . . And we are now telling *you* the good news, the occurrence of what the Fathers were promised" (13.27f,32). Like Peter in chapter 3, Paul is trying to leave every way open for his audience, not blaming them for what has happened. They, too, fail to respond. His appeal is no more successful than the prolonged campaign in Jerusalem, and he renounces the Jews, formally turning to the Gentiles. "It was necessary for the word of God to be first spoken to you. Since you reject it and deem yourselves unworthy of eternal life, see we turn to the Gentiles, for so the Lord has commanded us" (13.46f). It is no accident, as Dibelius has pointed out,[1] that a formal statement of rejection is delivered three times to the Jews of the Dispersion, once in each main area of mission: in Asia Minor, in Greece, and in Rome (18.6; 28.25–8). The last rejection sums up the verdict of God on all the Jews, a verdict painfully discovered by the Church throughout the whole of Acts: "Therefore let it be known to you that this salvation of God has been sent to the Gentiles; they will hear" (28.28). Whether Luke means this rejection of the Jews to be final in God's purpose, it is hard to say; certainly the conversion of the people as a whole is no longer to be considered by the Church as part of its mission (cf. 1.6f).[2]

---

[1] *Aufsätze*, 129; *Studies*, 149.

[2] Goppelt, op. cit., 231 n 3, says that Luke never indicates whether the "time of the Gentiles" will end with the conversion of Israel (Luke 21.24). It seems to me that this verse and Acts 1.6f; 3.19–21 do imply that Israel will return in the end, but Luke is at pains to stop speculation on this point; the immediate mission of the Church in history is to the Gentiles.

Stephen's speech is not aberrant. It is used by Luke to present an important element in his theology, and foreshadows the position to which God has driven the Church as a whole. In the context of Acts the speech is "a theoretical justification in advance for Christianity's turning away from the Jews to the Gentiles, made in terms of the stubbornness of the Jews. This is, from the point of view of the author of Acts, the chief purpose of the speech" (Overbeck).[1]

The speech as a whole fits into Luke's theological pattern, but it remains true that Stephen expresses his point of view in an extreme way, without the qualifications which the other historical characters in Acts must supply. He says that the Jews built the Temple under a misconception; they expected that God would dwell there whereas "the Most High does not dwell in things made with hands". What he does not say is that the Temple is a perfectly acceptable "house of prayer", as Jesus did, and as the Apostles showed they believed by their practice.

Two questions arise. Did the historic Stephen really put forward this uncompromising view of the Temple? When did this view of the Temple come to be accepted as part of a complete Christian theology of the destiny of the Jewish people? The only way to begin to answer these questions is to look for parallels in Jewish and Christian literature. The first parallel to Stephen's attack on a false theology of the Temple occurs in Acts itself. Paul on the Areopagus states that "the God who made the world and everything in it, he who is Lord of heaven and earth, does not live in shrines made with hands..." (17.24). This should warn us that Luke believes that Christian theology as a whole has repudiated the traditional Jewish view of the Temple, but it does not carry us much further in a search for parallels.

Jewish parallels have been brought forward from the writings preserved at Qumrân and from the literature of Hellenistic Judaism.

---

[1] Quoted by Joh. Weiss, *Ueber die Absicht und den literarischen charakter der Apg.* (Göttingen, 1897), 13; cf. Preuschen, *Die Apg., Hdb. z. N. T.* (Tübingen, 1913), 38.

The case for connecting the Qumrân sect with Stephen (and the so-called Hellenists) rests mainly on a passage in the Manual of Discipline ix.3–5, supported by a remark of Josephus about the Essenes, *Ant.* xviii.1.5.[1] The point of contact is supposed to be that both Stephen and the Qumrân sect denied the validity of Temple worship. Josephus, however, suggests something quite different: that the Essenes continued to send offerings to the Temple although they themselves kept away from it because of the laxity of the ritual observances. They made their own sacrifices separately. "When the Essenes send their gifts to the Temple, they do not offer sacrifices owing to a difference in rites of purity which they practice, and therefore being excluded from the common precinct (of the Temple), they offer sacrifices by themselves."[2]

The Damascus Document suggests a similar attitude to the Temple: reverence, combined with a horror of its present defilement, which leads the members of the covenant to forsake its ordinances.[3] Apart from the one passage in the Manual of Discipline mentioned above, the rest of the Qumrân literature suggests a similar position, a reverence for the priesthood and the Holy of Holies combined with a rigid standard of purity. The cited passage can, however, be translated in two ways, either to mean that sacrifices will be superseded and that atonement will be made in a better way than "by flesh of burnt offerings and fats of sacrifice", or to mean that a time

---

[1] O. Cullmann, "The Significance of the Qumrân Texts for Research into the Beginnings of Christianity", *J.B.L.*, 74 (1955), 213–26, reprinted in K. Stendahl, *The Scrolls and the N.T.* (London, 1958), 18–32. J. S. Johnson, "The Dead Sea Manual of Discipline and the Jerusalem Church of Acts", *Z.A.W.*, 66 (1954), 106–20, Stendahl op. cit., 129–42, is more cautious, and M. Simon, op. cit., 90f, rejects this point of contact, but it is hard to see what remains to justify saying that "the Qumrân sect was probably close to the Hellenists" (Simon). The Seven is too slight a connection.

[2] Tr. by F. M. Cross, *The Ancient Library of Qumrân and Modern Biblical Studies* (The Haskell Lectures, 1956–7) (London, 1958), 75f. Cross's book contains an excellent summary of the position, 74–7.

[3] J. M. Baumgarten, "Sacrifice and Worship among the Jewish Sectaries of the Dead Sea (Qumrân) Scrolls", *H.T.R.*, xlv (1952), 141–59; for the Damascus Document, especially 143–9.

will come when sacrifices are again acceptable to God. The latter translation is undoubtedly the correct one, and this passage now fits in with everything else that is known of the sect.[1] They are preparing for the time when pure and undefiled sacrifices will again be offered to God, and they cannot be cited as in any way displaying the sort of doctrine Stephen is expounding. Indeed, they would be completely opposed to each other.

The evidence for believing that some Jews of the Dispersion rejected the Temple and its sacrifices is found in two places, Justin's Dialogue with Trypho, 117.2, and the Sibylline Oracles, iv.8–12.[2] The first reports that Trypho interpreted Mal. 1.10–12 to mean that God had rejected the sacrifices offered in Jerusalem while accepting as sacrifices the prayers of the Jews in the Dispersion. This interpretation only arose after the Temple had been destroyed and it is impossible to regard it as a source of the historic Stephen's thought. The same is true of the passage from the Sibylline Oracles, which condemns in general the doctrine that God dwells in Temples: "For he has not as his habitation a stone set up in a temple."[3] The fourth book of the Sibyllines mentions both the destruction of Jerusalem and the eruption of Vesuvius in A.D. 79, and so cannot have been written at a time to influence Stephen.[4] It is hard to avoid the conclusion that such a doctrine could only arise in Hellenistic Judaism, where the Temple and the Holy City were so highly reverenced, after A.D. 70.

The Christian parallels to Stephen's view of the Temple are also to be found only after A.D. 70. They are contained in the

---

[1] Jean Carmignac, "L'utilité ou l'inutilité des sacrifices sanglants dans la 'Règle de la communauté' de Qumrân", *Revue Biblique*, lxiii (1956), 524–32 with a postscript by J. T. Milik. Carmignac and Milik produce parallels which show that the מן should be taken to denote origin rather than comparison.

[2] Quoted and discussed by M. Simon, "Saint Stephen and the Jerusalem Temple", *J.E.H.*, ii (1951), 127–42 at 136f; and op. cit., 84–90.

[3] Line 8; tr. H. C. O. Lanchester.

[4] See lines 115f, 125ff, and 130–6; R. H. Pfeiffer, *History of New Testament Times* (N.Y., 1949), 226–30.

Epistle of Barnabas (*c.* A.D. 135),[1] and the Pseudo-Clementines. The Epistle to the Hebrews scarcely needs to be considered, as it is more concerned with explaining what the Temple did signify than with denying that God dwelt in it.

The negative teaching about the Temple in the Epistle of Barnabas is an exact parallel to Stephen. The same passage in Isaiah is quoted to support the argument, which runs: "Further, I shall speak to you about the Temple, how those poor people were deceived and put their trust in the building, as though it was the house of God, and not in their God who made them. They were almost the same as the Gentiles in the way they hallowed him in the Temple." He then quotes Isa. 40.12 and 66.1 and concludes, "You know that their hope was vain" (16.1-2). The Epistle of Barnabas goes on to apply the O.T. passages about the Temple to believers, in whom God dwells, but this positive interpretation does nothing to weaken the complete correspondence between Stephen and the pseudonymous epistle on this one point.

The Pseudo-Clementine literature provides a number of parallels to Stephen's rejection of the Temple, though in view of Irenaeus's statement that the Ebionites "worshipped towards Jerusalem as though it was the house of God" (i.26.2) it would be rash to call these ideas "Ebionite".[2] The most striking parallel is in the Recognitions i.38: "But when the people sought men who were tyrants rather than kings, they also built a temple to satisfy royal ambition on the spot which had been predestined to them for prayer, and so, as godless kings followed one another, the people themselves sank into greater godlessness." Another parallel is to be found in the Homilies ii.44.1f, but again there is no ground for supposing that these ideas derive directly from a group within the primitive Church. In the latest study of the Pseudo-Clementines, by Georg Strecker, the passage from the Recognitions is ascribed to the Ἀναβαθμοὶ

---

[1] Windisch, *Hdb.z.N.T.* (Tübingen, 1920), 412; the Ep. Barn. was first dated at A.D. 130-1 by Schürer (1890); see Ladenze, "L'Épitre de Barnabé: la date de sa composition et son caractère général," *Revue d'histoire ecclésiastique*, i (1900), 31-60 and 212-25 for the full argument.

[2] M. Simon, art. cit., 140; op. cit., 113f.

Ἰακώβου (II, to be distinguished from I described by Epiphanius), which could not have been written before A.D. 150, and the second is ascribed to the *Kerygmata Petrou*, which probably belongs about A.D. 200.[1] Although these ideas are probably much older than the writings in which they appear, there is no reason to doubt the conclusion which all the other evidence has led us to accept, that it was the destruction of the Temple in A.D. 70 that released for the first time in both Judaism and Christianity a radical questioning of the dogma that God dwelt in the Temple.[2] There were abundant passages in the Prophets to seize on to support the attack, but in all the writings we have cited, with the possible exception of Rec. i.38, the new theology is worked out in terms borrowed from Hellenism.

However, the absence of parallels to Stephen's thought in the time he lived does not prove that the historic Stephen did not expound such ideas. He may have been an original thinker who was the first to take a new and bold step in Christian theology. The strongest argument for Stephen's originality lies in the fact that there is no reference in his speech to the destruction of the Temple in A.D. 70, though it is this event which seems to have precipitated that strain of thought in Hellenistic Judaism and in Jewish Christianity which repudiated the Temple cult. If Luke was composing the speech rather than reporting it, one would think, he could hardly have resisted mentioning the event which confirmed his argument.[3]

[1] *Das Judenchristentum in den Pseudoklementinen*, *T.U.*, v.15 (= 70. Band) (Berlin, 1958). The dating of the two sources is discussed on 253f and 219f. For the question of hostility to the Temple and the cult see especially 179–84.

[2] Cf. Strecker and G. Bornkamm's rejection of Schoeps's attempt to show that the Pseudo-Clementines contain documents which represent the genuine teaching of the apostolic age; *Z.K.G.*, lxiv (1952–53), 196–204.

[3] It might indeed be argued from this silence that Luke could not have known of the fall of Jerusalem, i.e. he was writing before A.D. 70. But if the Temple was still standing, Stephen's speech, by its round-about reply to the charge that Jesus would destroy the Temple, would leave very much in doubt the political respectability of the Church. Luke elsewhere is at great pains to clear the Church of all suspicion of trouble-making and he could easily have done so here, if it had been necessary. The conclusion must be that it was not necessary; the Temple had been destroyed and everyone knew that the Christians played no important part in the events.

The answer to this objection lies in the nature of Stephen's defence against the two charges. The essence of the defence was, as has been argued earlier, that the Jews were the law-breakers and the innovators. It was important that Stephen's claims should rest on one foundation, and one foundation alone: the will of God represented in the O.T. tradition. Any appeal to special prophetic knowledge about the future would weaken, if not deny, the substance of the defence. On the grounds of O.T. history, which came to a logical conclusion in the denial of the Messiah, the Jews were the ones who were guilty of these charges, not the Christians. The readers of Acts would of course know that a Jewish rebellion was finally responsible for the destruction of the Temple, but Luke wants them to understand that this too, like the sufferings of the Messiah, could be discerned from the O.T. alone. The absence of reference to the destruction of the Temple in Stephen's speech is not an indication that it represents a report of what was said at the martyrdom; it may well indicate just the opposite, and fits perfectly into the pattern of Luke's editorial intentions.

There may, however, have been a specifically Christian influence at work on Stephen, which could account for his radical theology of the Temple. This is the saying of Jesus reported by false witnesses, "I shall destroy this Temple . . .". That the Church preserved it, despite the opportunity it offered for misunderstanding, is an argument in favour of its authenticity. On the surface the saying could be responsible for Stephen's radical reinterpretation of Jewish history, but the difficulty seems to be that Jesus' saying implies that the Temple once had divine significance and that there must be a new temple to replace the old. Jesus has come to destroy and replace, like the Messiah in Enoch,[1] not to demonstrate that the Temple was never part of God's plan. No Jew, however hellenized he had become, would adopt the notion that the Temple had no divine significance simply under the influence

---

[1] Enoch 90.29. See Klostermann, *Das Markusevangelium, Hdb.z.N.T.* (4th ed., Tübingen, 1950), 155.

of this saying of Jesus. Even Philo gives the Temple a typological part in his theology, and it was not until the Temple was actually destroyed that room was made on the fringes of Diaspora Judaism for the sort of view which Stephen expounds.

It is impossible to be finally certain, but all the evidence shows that Stephen's theology of the Temple only arose after its destruction in A.D. 70. This is not the same as saying that Luke composed the speech out of his own head; on the contrary, he seems to have been using sources for his framework and, where he was forced to reconstruct, he did his best to give what a Hellenistic Jew[1] would have said. There is no doubt that Stephen was martyred and that Luke possessed an account of the lynching. The theology of the speech and even the wording also come in some way from a source or sources, though it is doubtful if those sources go back to Stephen. Haenchen, following up a suggestion made by Dibelius, has argued with some plausibility that the neutral parts of the account of Israel's history are copied from a Hellenistic Jewish source,[2] but even in the parts for which Luke is more directly responsible, where the two charges are being answered, we are still dealing with a historian and not a romancer. Luke is working within a Church tradition which had close contacts with Hellenistic Judaism, as we shall argue in Chapter Six. Professor Kilpatrick has provided detailed evidence that a closing phrase in Stephen's speech employed a messianic prophecy which was current in those circles, which is also found in 1 Clement, Polycarp, Irenaeus, and the Acta Philippi. It probably read: οἱ

---

[1] The meaning of the word ἑλληνιστής is still in dispute. Cadbury, *Beginnings*, v.59–74 at 71, is right in suggesting that the third instance, Acts 11.19f, should be taken as the starting point. (The reading of B E *614*, etc., should be preferred.) Here the word means "Greeks". In 6.1 and 9.29 it is clear that a longstanding division between Jews is involved (against Cadbury) which probably showed itself in the language they commonly spoke; the word still means "Greeks", though in the context it implies "Greek-speaking Jews". It had no pejorative force. Cf. C. F. D. Moule, "Once More, Who Were the Hellenists?" *E.T.*, lxx (1958–9), 100ff.

[2] Haenchen, op. cit., 245–7; cf. Cadbury, *The Book of Acts in History* (London, 1955), 102–4.

προφῆται ἐκήρυξαν (or προεκήρυξαν) τὴν ἔλευσιν τοῦ χριστοῦ.[1]
All the evidence suggests that Luke consciously adopted an
ancient theological tradition and clothed it in traditional
language, but it remains true that he is the master of the
material, and that the arguments used and the part the
martyrdom played in his account of how the gospel was rejected by the Jews and taken to the Gentiles are only fully
understood against a knowledge of his own theological purpose
in writing the history.

Acts presents a theology in which the Church has abandoned
the People and appropriated the Book.[2] The salvation of Israel
as a whole is no longer a living possibility, and the Church is
shown to be at last facing the destiny to which God was leading
it, by finally turning from the Jews to the Gentiles. Christian
theology did not come to this point of despair easily; it is
possible to discover the period in which the momentous change
took place and so obtain another indication of the historical
setting for the theology of Acts.

It is the enduring contribution of Professor Johannes Munck
to Pauline studies to have demonstrated that Paul's mission to
the Gentiles was no alternative to the mission to Israel.[3] His
argument may be briefly summarized as follows. Paul believed
that he had been called to preach to the Gentiles as a necessary
step towards the conversion of the Jews. Romans 9–11 is not an

---

[1] G. D. Kilpatrick, "Acts 7.52 ΕΛΕΥΣΙΣ", *J.T.S.*, xlvi (1945), 136–45.
Kilpatrick notes, 144, the paradox that though ἔλευσις is an earlier term
in logical theological development, in that it is used to avoid παρουσία
with its implication that the Messiah was on a level with God, it is found
in later Christian documents than those which contain παρουσία. In the
case of Acts 7, it may be suggested, there is no paradox to be explained,
since παρουσία would be an inappropriate term with which to describe
the Messiah's first coming. παρουσία is not used in that sense until Ign.
Philad. 9.2 and possibly 2 Pet. 1.16. The survival of the term ἔλευσις may
have been due to this appropriateness to the first coming; its use is not
evidence that a more primitive Christology is being preserved in Acts 7.

[2] Cf. Goppelt, op. cit., 228–31.

[3] "Israel and the Gentiles in the N.T.", *J.T.S.*, N.S. ii (1951), 3–16;
*Paulus und die Heilsgeschichte* (Acta Jutlandica, xxvi, Aarhus, 1954) Eng. tr.,
*Paul and the Salvation of Mankind* (London, 1959); *Christus und Israel; eine
Auslegung von Röm.* 9–11 (Acta Jutlandica, xxviii, Aarhus, 1956).

insignificant piece of self-justification, but the key to Paul's understanding of his mission. What divided Paul and the earliest Apostles was not a conflict between an exclusive desire to keep the gospel for Israel and a doctrine of universalism, but a difference of emphasis: the earliest Apostles were working with Israel for Israel and the Gentiles, whose salvation would follow the conversion of the Jews, while Paul was working with the Gentiles for the Gentiles and Israel. Paul vehemently denied that God had rejected his people; "I do not want you to be ignorant of this mystery, brethren, in case you become conceited", he wrote; "a partial hardening has come over Israel until the fullness of the gentiles shall have come in, and in this way all Israel will be saved" (Rom. 11.25f). The question of the salvation of Israel has not been excluded from the discussion as it has in Luke-Acts, and Paul is constantly working with this end in mind. It is true that two verses in 1 Thessalonians (2.14–16) seem to contradict all that has been said: whatever the precise sense of εἰς τέλος in the last sentence, ἔφθασεν δὲ ἐπ' αὐτοὺς ἡ ὀργὴ εἰς τέλος, it does not offer much hope for the Jews. But these two verses cannot be pitted against the three chapters in Romans as representing Paul's considered view of the destiny of his own people; either they are not his genuine words, or they represent a justifiable outburst of anger with no serious theological implications, or they state only one side of the paradox which is to be fully expounded in Romans.[1] We may conclude that, if the salvation of Israel was a central concern for St Paul, it was much more the central concern of all parts of the early Church. Despite the hostility of the Jews towards the Christians, the Church continued to work for their redemption.

After A.D. 70 Jewish hostility towards the Church increased and steps were taken to exclude Christians from the synagogues. The Gospel according to St Matthew reflects the point of view of a Church which has been forced to define its opposition to

[1] The first explanation is that of the Tübingen school; for the second see Jülicher-Fascher, *Einleitung* (7th ed., Tübingen, 1931), 61f; for the third see Goppelt, op. cit., 112–25 and *passim*.

Judaism and its mission to the Gentiles without finally abandoning the hope that Israel would repent. The opposition between the Church and Pharisaism is still seen as an opposition within Judaism.[1] The Didache, which belongs to a similar tradition, shows the process taken to the point when the breach is open and irrevocable. The Jews are now simply "the hypocrites", whose religious behaviour the Church must on no account follow (8.1–3).[2]

Both Matthew and the Didache, however, have come to their position in debate with Rabbinic Judaism, from which they have both learnt so much. The Lucan position has closer affinities with the Epistle of Barnabas and the writings of Aristides and Justin Martyr, where Rabbinic tradition is unimportant. The traditional methods of expounding the Septuagint which they have taken over from Hellenistic Judaism show that this is the principal influence. The Epistle of Barnabas explains the breaking of the tablets of the Law by Moses as the final breach of the covenant.[3] From that point onwards the Jewish history is no longer the history of God's covenant with his people, and the significance of the records of this history in the O.T. lies solely in the fact that they foretell Christ and provide lessons for the Church. The Apology of Aristides, which perhaps belongs to the same period, puts the Jews almost on the same level as the heathen; they think that they are worshipping God, but in fact they only worship the angels.[4] In Justin Martyr the O.T. has become a book of riddles to which the right answer in every case is Jesus the Messiah, and his long and patient dialogue with Trypho the Jew is principally concerned with showing that this is true. There is no sense that Jews and Christians share a common history; what they possess in common is a religious book which the Christians understand and the Jews do not.[5] Justin's special efforts to convert Trypho

---

[1] See G. D. Kilpatrick, *The Origins of the Gospel according to St Matthew* (2nd ed., Oxford, 1950), especially chapter VI; Goppelt, op. cit., 178–85.

[2] Goppelt, ibid., 186–9.     [3] Ep. Barn. 4.6–8; 14.1–5.

[4] Apol. Aristides 14, Syrian text, tr. by J. Rendel Harris, *The Apology of Aristides* (Cambridge, 1891), 48; cf. the Greek text.

[5] Goppelt, op. cit., 284–301, especially 288.

do not seem to spring from a view that it is more important to convert Jews than Gentiles; the only difference is that it is harder. Justin believes that Christians are bound to refute all men who contradict the Scriptures, on pain of being judged guilty of negligence at the day of judgement, and it is for this general reason that he conducts the dialogue with a Jew.[1]

The general position which the Church had reached in its relations with the Jews may be summed up in Ignatius's dictum: "For Christianity has not based its faith on Judaism, but Judaism on Christianity, into which has been gathered every tongue that believes in God" (Magn. 10.3).[2] The prophets of the O.T. "lived according to Christ Jesus", and so Judaism is a misguided derivative from Christianity (Magn. 8.2; 9.2).[3]

Acts stands in this tradition. It traces back to the apostolic age the rejection of the gospel by the Jews. It shows how the People, despite all the efforts of the early Christian preachers and the persuasiveness of their arguments from Scripture, rejected the gospel; it argues that this rejection was long ago foretold in the Book, to which Christians alone—pious men like Stephen—now hold the key. The Lucan interpretation of the history of the establishment of the Church reflects a theology which developed in the second century, and all the elements which go to make up his story, though they are derived from a variety of traditional sources, must be seen in relation to the standpoint of a second-century theologian.

[1] Dial. 82.3f; 38.2; 44.1; see Harnack, *Judentum und Judenchristentum in Justins Dialog mit Trypho*, *T.U.*, iii.9 (=39. Band) (Leipzig, 1913), 82–4.
[2] Cf. K. Lake's tr. (Loeb Classical Library, London, 1912).
[3] Bauer, *Hdb.z.N.T.*, *Ergänzungsband* (Tübingen, 1920), 228.

# CHAPTER FOUR

## JEWISH CHRISTIANS AND
## GENTILE CHRISTIANS

IN THE last chapter it has been argued that the theology of Acts consists not so much in the doctrines which are put into the mouths of the chief historical characters as in the movement of the history. God was leading the Church to understand his will in its historical experience, as it was driven out of Jerusalem and towards Rome. For that reason it is more important in studying the theology of Acts to investigate the history of the developing relationship between groups—between the Church and the Jews, and between Jews and Gentiles within the Church—than the classical doctrinal questions like the relationship between Gospel and Law.

The present question, that of the agreement reached concerning the status of Jews and Gentiles in the Church, has in fact been taken by the Tübingen school as the key to the purpose of Acts. In 1836 Schrader and F. C. Baur revived the hypothesis that Acts was an attempt to reconcile the supporters of Paul and the Judaizers by making Paul as Petrine and Peter as Pauline as possible.[1] Few scholars would now accept Baur's picture of the early Church, divided into Judaizers led by Peter and universalists led by Paul, but, leaving that question aside for the moment, his thesis remains important because it raises the issue: what was Luke's theological purpose in presenting the historical discussion of the steps by which Gentiles were admitted into the full fellowship of the Church in the way he did?

This problem can only be avoided if it can be shown that

[1] See the admirable summary by A. C. McGiffert, *Beginnings*, ii.367–9.

Luke is writing an accurate account of the meetings which were held and the decisions which were taken by the Apostles and the Jerusalem Church in consultation with Paul and Barnabas. That is no longer possible. This does not mean that Acts is historically worthless. It is still necessary to correlate the historical data presented in Acts with the other extant accounts, particularly with the opening chapters of Galatians, in the continuing search for the historical truth of the matter, but the present results of that investigation show that Acts is mistaken at one point or another. If Acts is mistaken, we must ask why Luke was able to give such a clear and definite account of the outcome of the discussions; he lacked precise historical information and yet he has felt bound to record a decisive debate with a definite conclusion. Acts remains a most important source-book for the history of the early Church, but the inaccuracies in such a clear account must lead us to suspect that the author's assurance springs from knowing his own mind rather than from possessing circumstantial knowledge of the mind of the Apostles.

Without discussing again all the suggestions which have been made to reconcile the accounts of Paul's visits to Jerusalem in Galatians and Acts, we must support the assertion that there are at least some inaccuracies in Luke's version. Many scholars are prepared to admit this; they argue that Luke has presented two accounts (Acts 11 and 15) of the one visit (Gal. 2.1ff),[1] or that Acts 15 is an account of a meeting which either occurred elsewhere[2] or which Paul did not attend,[3] or they adopt some other "imaginative reconstruction".[4] There remain the two classical solutions by which the accuracy of Acts would remain unimpaired. J. B. Lightfoot has argued that the coincidences between Acts 15 and Gal. 2.1ff in point of geography, time,

---

[1] J. Wellhausen, E. Schwarz, P. Wendland, Preuschen, Bousset, Loisy, E. Meyer, Windisch, Bultmann, Goguel.

[2] E.g., Lake, *Beginnings*, v.199–204.

[3] E.g., J. N. Sanders, *N.T.S.*, ii (1955), 133–43 at 141.

[4] The phrase is C.S.C. Williams's. See his survey in *A Commentary on the Acts of the Apostles*, Black's N.T. Commentaries (London, 1957), 24–30.

persons involved, subject of dispute, the character of the conference, and its result are so close as to render the differences unimportant. "A combination of circumstances so striking is not likely to have occurred twice within a few years."[1] The difficulties in this view, however, are very great. Not only are there important differences between the two accounts of the Jerusalem consultation, but it is impossible to believe that Paul would not have mentioned in Galatians his earlier visit to Jerusalem recorded in Acts 11—if the omission was discovered, his whole case would have been imperilled—and it is difficult to imagine Peter and James behaving in the way they did over Peter's eating with Gentile Christians in Antioch if they had just promulgated the Jerusalem Decree in the Acts version. In whatever way the objections are met, the reliability of Acts can scarcely be maintained by this solution.

The other classical solution is Sir William Ramsay's.[2] He supposes that there were, as Acts says, two journeys (Acts 11 and 15), and that the private consultation recorded in Gal. 2.1–10 took place during the first, the famine-relief visit. The two chief difficulties of this view are that it leaves very little room for the fourteen (much less seventeen years) which Paul says had elapsed since his conversion, even if one puts the famine visit as late as A.D. 48, and that it raises the problem of why Galatians now contains no mention of the visit described in Acts 15, a visit which had important results for Paul's case. The second objection is the more serious one, and the only way it can be met without damaging the credibility of Acts is to suppose that Galatians was written before the council had taken place and was, therefore, the earliest of the letters of St Paul. This has always seemed an unlikely supposition on grounds of style, but not until recently has anyone stated the objections in an

---

[1] *St Paul's Epistle to the Galatians* (10th ed., London, 1890), 123–8; the quotation is on 124. This position is supported by Wendt, Baumgarten, Blass, Joh. Weiss, Wikenhauser, Dupont, Cullmann, Bo Reicke.

[2] *St Paul the Traveller and the Roman Citizen* (London, 1895). This solution is supported by Emmet, Burkitt, Cadoux, Duncan, W. L. Knox, F. F. Bruce, C. S. C. Williams. Bruce, *New London Commentary* (London, 1954), 301 n 10, points out that Calvin advanced this view in 1548.

objectively convincing manner. C. H. Buck[1] has now pointed out that when the style of Galatians is compared with that of 2 Cor. 1–9 and Romans it is clear that Galatians was written late and not early. His argument is that, though the antithesis "spirit–flesh" occurs in all three letters, the antithesis "faith–works" is absent from 2 Cor. 1–9, the terms being used separately in a non-technical sense. The pairs "faith and works", "spirit and flesh" are combined in both Galatians and Romans. "If Paul had already written Galatians, is it conceivable that he could, at some later time, have written 2 Cor. 1–9, with its vehement anti-legal position, without once employing the antithesis, faith–works?"[2] Lightfoot's objection to Ramsay's theory seems to be sustained.

Baur and the early members of the Tübingen school deduced from the fact that Luke's account of the negotiations was inexact the conclusion that he had deliberately constructed a tendentious narrative in order to reconcile the opposing parties. It was soon pointed out by Baur's younger followers that it was very improbable that the author of Acts would have been aware of what he was doing, and have deliberately falsified the story of the events to produce a compromise. If the supposed two parties were still conscious of the points of disagreement, any attempt to blur the issue would be bound to fail; it is much more likely that Luke wrote at a time when the original debates had been forgotten.[3] This is a likely hypothesis, but it requires rigorous testing in order to be sustained, for it is still possible that Luke's inaccuracy was due only to a slip of memory or a momentary confusion over the facts. We shall test it by setting out as uncontroversially as possible the events affecting the status of Jews and Gentiles in the Church, in the first place as they can be inferred from Paul's Epistles and then as they can be inferred from Acts.

Three statements can be made on the basis of the Epistle to

---

[1] "The Date of Galatians", *J.B.L.*, lxx (1951), 113–22.    [2] Ibid., 121.

[3] E.g., A. Ritschl, "Das Verhältniss der Schriften des Lukas zu der Zeit ihrer Entstehung", *Theologische Jahrbücher*, vi (1847), 293–304 at 300; and cf. Overbeck.

the Galatians, although their precise meaning and the implications to be drawn from them are still vigorously disputed.

First, it was agreed in Jerusalem between James, Peter, John, Paul, and Barnabas that Peter was called to exercise an apostleship to the circumcised and Paul an apostleship to the Gentiles (Gal. 2.7–10). Second, probably a little later,[1] envoys (or an envoy)[2] came from James in Jerusalem to Antioch and caused Peter and Barnabas to withdraw from eating with Gentile Christians. Third, Paul was up against Judaizers in the Galatian Church and had also been set upon in Jerusalem by some men who considered themselves Christians (though Paul calls them "false brethren") who tried to force him to circumcise Titus. The logic of Paul's argument shows that Paul connected the group in Jerusalem with the Judaizers in Galatia,[3] but it may be that one lot were Jews and the other Gentiles;[4] we cannot assume the existence of an organized party and certainly should reject the idea that they were supported by James or Peter.[5]

These three statements may seem straightforward, but it is very difficult to draw many certain implications from them. What do they imply about the question of Jews and Gentiles eating together, and what do they imply about circumcision? Strangely enough, the agreement reached at Jerusalem cannot have included or even implied a definite line of policy on the rules governing fellowship at table between Jews and Gentiles; if it had, the subsequent trouble at Antioch would have been avoided. Perhaps the division of apostolic tasks between Peter and Paul was made at a time when Gentile converts were so few that the problem of social intercourse with their fellow

---

[1] Munck, *Paulus und die Heilsgeschichte* (Aarhus, 1954), 92–5, Eng. tr., *Paul and the Salvation of Mankind* (London, 1959), 100–3, makes an unconvincing attempt to argue that it was earlier.

[2] See the discussion by T. W. Manson, *B.J.R.L.*, xxiv (1940), 69f.

[3] Loisy, *L'Épître aux Galates* (Paris, 1916), 111.

[4] The question turns on the interpretation of Gal. 6.13, οἱ περιτεμνόμενοι αὐτοί.

[5] J. H. Ropes, *The Singular Problem of the Epistle to the Galatians* (Cambridge, Mass., 1929), 44f.

Jewish Christians had not yet arisen. It may also be that the
general Jewish attitude to the problem had not yet hardened,
as it was to do in the '50's when the Zealots became prominent
in Jewish politics.[1]

The question of circumcision is even more puzzling. The
agreement itself says nothing explicit about what shall be
required from the Gentiles who believe through Paul's apostleship. That explains why he has to bring forward two negatives
to prove that the Jerusalem leaders did not require circumcision; he cannot cite a positive ruling, but he can point to the
fact that Titus was not compelled to be circumcised and that
the "Pillars" "added nothing to him" (ἐμοὶ . . . προσανέθεντο),
asking "only" that he remember the poor. This absence of a
positive ruling also explains the fact that the problem of circumcision is still a live issue in Paul's later letters, which would be surprising if an authoritative pronouncement had ever been made.[2]

It has often been suggested, however, that the question of
circumcision was even less settled than that, because eventually
Titus was circumcised. The argument turns on the omission by
D*, vg(1), Iren.[lat], Tert., Ambst., Pelag., of the words οἷς
οὐδὲ in Gal. 2.5; it then proceeds to re-interpret verse 3 to
mean, "Titus was not *compelled* to be circumcised (but neverthe-
less he agreed to it of his own free will)." There are many
objections to this argument, but two seem to be decisive. The
first is Kirsopp Lake's: "Paul might have admitted that he
'yielded', but never that his yielding was a 'subjection'."[3] The
second is made by Lietzmann: "And supposing the original
text had read πρὸς ὥραν εἴξαμεν, it is understandable that an

---

[1] Bo Reicke, "Der geschichtliche Hintergrund des Apostelkonzils und
der Antiochia-Episode, Gal. 2.1–14", *Studia Paulina* in honour of de Zwaan
(Haarlem, 1953), 172–87 at 182ff. He suggests that Gal. 2.12, τοὺς ἐκ
περιτομῆς refers to these Zealots, and that James had to yield to Zealot
pressure if he was not to forfeit all influence with his own people.

[2] T. W. Manson, op. cit., 77.

[3] Op. cit., 31f n 10. The words τῇ ὑποταγῇ are omitted by p[46]. Perhaps
this is the original text, and the words were added to allow for the circumcision of Timothy (Acts 16.3), which was done freely; note then that the
original text must have stated that Titus was not circumcised, if the
addition was to have had any point.

οὐδέ might have been added, but not an οἶς, which needlessly changes a smooth construction into an intolerable anocoluthon."[1] We conclude that Titus was not circumcised and that Paul relies on the absence of any such demand by the Jerusalem authorities in his argument with the Judaizers in Galatia—but he has to rely on this negative sort of argument, backed by his recognized apostolic authority, because no positive ruling on the question had ever been given.

The Book of Acts also provides information on each of the three points we have deduced from Galatians, on apostolic strategy, on table-fellowship, and on the activities of Judaizers.

First, the apostolic strategy in Acts is completely singleminded.[2] The book is not divided into two parts: "home missions" and "foreign missions", the work of Peter and the work of Paul. The gospel increases and spreads in one direction, from Jerusalem to the ends of the earth, and Peter and Paul with a host of lesser characters only appear on the stage to illustrate this one movement. Even the central position given to the city of Jerusalem, a constant element which might seem to contradict the dominant trend, serves it in a special way; Jerusalem is the rallying point from which further advances are made. The action is held back to allow Peter to convert the first Gentile, the centurion Cornelius,[3] and then it plunges on to the missionary work among the Greeks in Antioch (11.20)[4] and to Paul's apprenticeship in that city for his work in Asia Minor, Greece, and Rome. Acts is silent about any agreement to divide the apostolic spheres of activity. It implies that vigorous missionary work was going on among the Jews at the same time as the gospel was spreading throughout the Gentile world (21.20), but it is not interested in that work for its own sake, and certainly does not particularly associate Peter with it.

[1] *Galaterbrief, Hdb.z.N.T.* (2nd ed., Tübingen, 1923), 11.
[2] See Chapter Two above.
[3] The status of the Ethiopian Treasurer is deliberately left vague; Haenchen, op. cit., 271.
[4] The correct reading here is ἑλληνιστάς, B E *614* cf. א; the unusual word has been changed to the more usual, and the context demands that it should mean "Greeks"; Ropes, *Beginnings*, iii.106.

Second, in Acts the question of table-fellowship is settled at the very beginning of any missionary activity among the Gentiles by Peter's vision and his visit to Cornelius. Those meat regulations which make a distinction between clean and unclean animals are abolished as a prelude to the Gentile mission, and the abolition of this distinction is regarded as symbolic of the abolition of the distinction between men (10.28; 11.3, etc.). The so-called Apostolic Decree in Acts 15 does not reopen the question, nor does it, in the eyes of Luke, bring back any of the distinctions which have been abolished. The council affirms the position which the Jerusalem Church had already adopted after hearing Peter's report of the conversion of Cornelius (11.18). The Gentile Christians are recognized (by all except a group of converted Pharisees) as full members of the Church, and the council is chiefly concerned with deciding which parts of the Law are applicable to them. Because Cornelius has already received the Holy Spirit without being circumcised, circumcision obviously cannot be required, and the analogy of the observances laid down for the "stranger within the gate" in Lev. 17 and 18 is invoked to provide the four cultic requirements of the Decree.[1] The preservation of table-fellowship is not the reason for these regulations—at least Luke does not say that it is, and gives another more general ground for their adoption: they must be observed "because Moses has had men to proclaim him from time immemorial in every city; he has been read every Sabbath in the synagogues" (15.21). In other words, Moses is the universal Law-giver and the Gentiles have always possessed witnesses to that fact, whether they have recognized it or not.[2] The Gentiles are bound to observe the relevant parts of the Mosaic Law, even

[1] Ritschl, op. cit., 301; Loisy, *Les Actes des Apôtres* (Paris, 1920), 594; Waitz, *Z.K.G.*, lv (1936), 227–31.

[2] Loisy, op. cit., 595, perhaps pushes this too far, but he is substantially correct. "The speech means that these restrictions ought to be and can be imposed on the Gentiles because the Gentiles are familiar with the Law through the teaching of the synagogues; it means, too, that they do not disregard these restrictions, and that they also know that these restrictions concern them just as much as the Jews." Cf. the three interpretations put forward, *Beginnings*, iv.177f, none of which is satisfactory.

including these less obvious customs about food and marriage, because God has always intended Moses to be the Law-giver for all nations. It may be a minor point, but it should be noted that there is no suggestion that the distinction between clean and unclean animals should be re-introduced. The regulation touches only the method of preparing the meat, whatever the meat may be, provided of course that it has not been offered to idols. Table-fellowship is not the issue, but the question concerning what parts of the ceremonial Law should apply to Gentile Christians. This is confirmed by the mention of πορνεία, which refers to the prohibited degrees of marriage in Lev. 18[1] and would have no effect on table-fellowship. Admittedly the observance of the regulations in the Decree would make sharing meals between Jewish and Gentile Christians easier, but Luke has made it clear in the story of Cornelius that God has already removed that sort of barrier as the prelude to the Gentile mission, and that the later regulations are designed to meet the larger problems of the validity of the Mosaic Law in the Gentile parts of the Church.

Third, Acts knows of no Judaizers in the Church outside of Judea. Peter is required to justify his eating with Cornelius by "those of the circumcision" in Jerusalem (11.2); envoys from Judea stir up trouble in Antioch by teaching that Gentile Christians should be circumcised (15.1); and when Paul and Barnabas go up to Jerusalem to complain, they are challenged there by a group of Pharisees who had become Christians (15.5). Acts makes it quite clear, however, that each of these attempts to impose the strictest Jewish customs on Gentiles is decisively rejected and never supported for a moment by the leaders of the Jerusalem Church, including James. Paul, for his part, never countenances the demand that Jewish Christians should give up their Jewish religious customs. Even though a case could be made out for leaving Timothy uncircumcised—his father was a Greek—Paul did not hesitate to circumcise him, and later on he willingly adopted James's suggestion that he sponsor a group of Jews in their purification rites in order

---

[1] Loisy, ibid., 594.

to demonstrate to the Jewish Christians that he did not advocate the abandonment of the full Mosaic Law by Jews living
in the Dispersion (21.21).

The numerous attempts to solve the problems raised by the
chronological discrepancies between Acts and Galatians have
often masked the assumption that the general situation of Jews
and Gentiles in the Church is the same in both books. Any
differences, it is argued, can be explained by the fact that Paul
was writing in the heat of controversy while Luke could afford
to be more objective and calm, having seen a successful issue
to the disputes. A comparison of what Acts and Galatians say
on each of the three points will show that the differences are
greater than can be removed by that explanation. Acts presupposes a new and different situation.

Even the one crucial point on which both accounts agree,
that Gentile Christians need not be circumcised, is stated
differently. Paul cannot fall back simply on an authoritative
ruling from Jerusalem and is forced to use a variety of arguments in Galatians and elsewhere to repel the Judaizers who
said that Gentile Christians should be circumcised. In Acts it
is always made clear that circumcision for the Gentiles is
absolutely out of the question.[1] The significance of this difference appears more clearly when we turn to the other points.

On the question of apostolic strategy we have already
admitted that Acts provides enough information to deduce that
the Judean Church was carrying on a vigorous mission among
Jews at the same time as Paul and others were having such
success in the Gentile world (21.20). What is significant is the
lack of theological weight which is given to this mission to the
Jews. The plain meaning of the agreement cited by Paul in
Gal. 2.6–10 is that two "apostleships" are recognized, one to
the Jews under Peter, and the other to the Gentiles under Paul,
and it seems that the former is more important in the eyes of
the Mother Church than the latter. Most commentators avoid
taking account of the plain meaning of the agreement because

[1] Joh. Weiss, *Ueber die Absicht und den literarischen Charakter der Apg.*
(Göttingen, 1897), 26.

they find it impossible to give any practical significance to the terms of the division: there is no simple geographical division which would leave the Jews to Peter and the Gentiles to Paul, nor is it easy to see how Paul could avoid preaching to Jews as he went on his missionary journeys. They conclude that the meaning of the agreement is simply that the Jerusalem Church recognized Paul's right to conduct a Gentile mission without imposing circumcision of his converts, and they place the emphasis on the last part, the removal of the burden of circumcision.[1] We have already pointed out that Paul was forced to rely on negative arguments, on the absence of any demands in Jerusalem, and it is scarcely possible that he would have done so if he could have made his point by expressing the terms of the agreement a little more clearly. The agreement must be taken at its face value. The leaders of the Church were asked by Paul to recognize that God had called him to carry on a new apostolic venture to the Gentiles alongside of their own mission to the Jews. We have already referred to Johannes Munck's interpretation of Romans 9–11, and it offers an equally satisfactory explanation here. He argues that the original Jewish Christians believed that their first and primary task was to convert their own people, and that the salvation of the rest of the world depended on the return of the Jews. Paul, on the other hand, held that "because of the unbelief and hardening of the Jews, God had ordained that the Gospel should be proclaimed to the Gentiles. This missionary activity would in turn eventually have its effect on the Jews through their envy of the believing Gentiles, when they saw that the Gentiles had obtained what was promised to Israel. Paul proclaimed, with a confidence which we do not find in the Gospel traditions or Acts in their present form, that the full salvation of the Gentiles should inaugurate the salvation of all Israel."[2] Even if the details of the interpretation should not find common assent, Munck is surely right to hold us to the terms of the agreement in Galatians; whatever the theology behind the division of

[1] E.g., Haenchen, op. cit., 413f.
[2] Op. cit., 270f; Eng. tr., 276.

apostolic function, it means that Paul has succeeded in getting
James, Peter, and John to recognize his right to conduct a full-
scale mission to the Gentiles independent of their own
campaign to win the Jews.

There is not enough evidence to decide whether the Jerusalem leaders ever despaired of their own attempts or supplemented them by a mission to the Gentiles, but clearly the
destruction of Jerusalem, the scattering of the Jews, and the
reduction to insignificance of the exiled Palestinian Jewish
Christians gave decisive significance to Paul's eccentric experi-
ment. The God of history vindicated his apostle, and it requires
an immense effort of historical imagination and access to Paul's
own writings to think ourselves back behind the events of
A.D. 70 and to understand the temerity of the man who knew
himself called to preach principally to Gentiles. The author of
Acts did not lack historical imagination, but in this case he was
not in a position to employ it to portray the true situation. Not
only did he have no access to Paul's correspondence, the indis-
pensable evidence, but he was also limited by his own purpose.
Knowing the judgement of God in history, his aim was to
proclaim that the present situation was the result of what the
Holy Spirit had been working out in the Church's life since the
earliest days. The mission to the Gentiles was to him not an
unorthodox diversionary operation, authorized at the insistence
of a brilliant subordinate commander, but the inevitable and
unmistakable direction of the campaign, in which all the
leaders had played their part from the beginning. Jesus himself
had foretold that the Jews would reject them and that they
would have to go to the Gentiles, who would hear (Luke 4.24–8;
Acts 1.8), and Luke's exposition of the divine scheme had no
place for two plans of campaign. The activities of all the
apostles illustrate the one movement, from Jerusalem to Rome.[1]

The case of the regulations governing table-fellowship also

---

[1] Cf. Overbeck's remark about Paul: "The Apostle of the Gentiles (Gal.
1.16; 2.7) has become a universal Apostle", *Introduction to De Wette's Commentary* (Eng. tr., London, 1875), 29; and M. Kiddle, "The Admission of
the Gentiles in St Luke's Gospel and Acts", *J.T.S.*, xxxvi (1935), 160–73.

provides indications of the situation in which the author of Acts is writing. It has often been remarked that it would be difficult for Peter to have behaved in the way he did in Antioch if the Decree of Acts 15 had already been issued, but it is less often noticed that it would have been even more difficult for him to behave as he did if he still remembered his vision of the clean and unclean animals in Acts 10. Acts regards the removal of the Jewish distinction between meats as the symbolic justification for the Gentile mission, while in Galatians it seems to be an unforeseen difficulty which arose only after the Gentile mission had been in operation for some time. This contradiction may be surmounted by supposing that Peter was never clear about the implications of the vision and that pressure from strict Jews became much stronger as time went on, but it remains strange that the Decree of Acts 15, which seems to solve the problem, should never be mentioned by Paul. Paul considers the question of whether Christians should eat meat which had been offered to idols in 1 Cor. 8.1–13 (cf. Rom. 14.13—15.13), and he never betrays by even a hint that the matter had been authoritatively decided in Jerusalem. There are two attempts to avoid concluding that he had never heard of such a decree. The first supposes that a regulation designed to govern relationships between Jewish and Gentile Christians would be inapplicable to a purely Gentile Church, but even if purely Gentile Churches did exist, the Jewish part of the Church as a whole would still be scandalized by the practice of eating meat offered to idols, and would certainly be justified in complaining that the Decree was accepted by Paul as a universal regulation to be applied throughout the Church. The second supposes that the Decree had been used as a basis of attack on Paul, and his assent to it had been taken as a sign that he was more dependent on Jerusalem than he would like to admit; that consequently he felt justified in ignoring it.[1] This argument might just suffice to explain Paul's silence about the Decree in Romans and 1 Corinthians, though it would do so at the expense of making Paul break a solemn piece of

[1] T. W. Manson, op. cit., 78.

"canon law", but it will not explain the silence of Galatians (which was written after the Decree had been made). If the Decree had been used to attack Paul's claims that he was independent of Jerusalem in his apostolic authority, to remain silent on the point, when he is arguing with special reference to his visits to the city, would be to wreck his case. Paul cannot have known about the Decree when he wrote 1 Corinthians, Galatians, and Romans. The simplest way to avoid this difficulty is to suppose that Luke was mistaken when he reported that Paul was present at the council in Acts 15, and that it is later implied that Paul first heard of the matter on his last visit to Jerusalem in Acts 21.[1] The difficulties in this view will become apparent when we consider the significance of the Decree in the Church in Luke's day.

In general the relationship between Jews and Gentiles in the Church in Acts seems to be dominated by questions of cultic observances. The problem of table-fellowship is solved in principle before the first Gentile is converted, and the problem of circumcision is met by imposing four requirements relating to food and marriage as the most that should be demanded of Gentile Christians. The Paul of the Epistles seems unhappily excluded from these comfortable solutions. He has to fight for the principle of table-fellowship even after the Gentile mission has been fully authorized by the Jerusalem leaders; he was never freed from the necessity of doing theological battle to show that the circumcision of Gentiles was an abandonment of loyalty to Christ; and he was unable to appeal to regulations which would provide a simple answer to the problem of whether to eat meat which had been offered to idols.

The situation implied in Acts becomes plain when the third point, the rôle of the Judaizers, is considered. The Judaizers seem to have been active in a number of Churches under Paul's care and his Epistles show that he was never able to forget their threat to the gospel. In Acts the only demands that Gentiles should become Jews when they became Christians

---

[1] J. N. Sanders, op. cit., 139f. The argument is rejected by F. F. Bruce, *The Acts of the Apostles* (London, 1951), 393f.

come from trouble-makers in Jerusalem. What is more important than this geographical restriction is that these demands are
immediately and uncompromisingly rejected. The Judaizers in
Acts never look like winning. James never draws the Jews back
from fellowship with Gentiles; Paul never has to fight against
false brethren who try to get Titus circumcised; and every
claim the Judaizers make is quickly and authoritatively
rejected.

The events which occurred when Paul returned to Jerusalem
for the last time provide the clue to Luke's understanding of
the problem.[1] James and the other Jerusalem leaders, speaking
corporately, say that disquieting rumours are abroad about
him and ask, in view of the large number of Jews zealous for
the Law who have become Christians, that he would do something to show that he is not teaching Jews in the Dispersion to
apostasize from Moses (21.20–5). They conclude by recapitu-
lating the terms of the agreement reached, as recorded in Acts
15. The repetition of the terms of the Decree has been taken
as an indication that Paul was hearing them for the first time,
but even if a source implying this did lie behind the speech—
and we have never found any signs that Luke possessed such
long and connected sources—we should still be left with the
question of why Luke repeated words which he believed Paul
had heard years before and had carried to other churches. The
answer lies in the peculiar nature of the whole request. Paul
was being asked to reassure the Jewish Christians that he had
never taught that they should abandon the Law. The Decree
is cited with a new and surprising force; it had been drafted to
protect Gentiles from demands that they should become full
Jews, but now it is invoked to guarantee to the Jews their rights
in the bargain to go on enforcing circumcision among themselves. It is beside the point to try to decide from such passages
as Gal. 5.2 and 1 Cor. 7.18f what ruling Paul would have
given on the question of whether Jewish Christians should go
on circumcizing their children; he was never asked, and the

[1] Overbeck, "Ueber das Verhältniss Justins des Märtyrers zur Apg.",
*Zeitschrift für wissenschaftliche Theologie*, xv (Leipzig, 1872), 335f.

Jewish Christians of his day would probably have regarded his judgement as irrelevant. Acts implies a different situation, where Gentile Christians were the dominant part of the Church and where the Jewish Christians were eager to obtain from them guarantees for the preservation of the practices they continued to demand from their own members. The author of Acts believed that the working arrangement between Jews and Gentiles in the Church should be maintained whereby neither side attempted to impose its views on the other. The seal of this agreement was the abstinence of the Gentile Church from food offered to idols, meat with the blood in it, animals which had been strangled, and the forbidden degrees of marriage. In return, the Gentile Church would protect the rights of Jewish Christians to maintain the Mosaic Law among its members as far as that was possible.

There is no evidence, in Paul or elsewhere, for the existence of such a *modus vivendi* before A.D. 70. Acts seems to presuppose a situation where the Jewish Christians were in a position in which they could be imagined asking for the protection of Paul's authority, and we must now ask whether there is evidence that the question was debated in these terms after the fall of Jerusalem.[1]

The Epistle of Ignatius to the Philadelphians 6.1 provides us with the first clue. "If any one discourses to you on Judaism, do not listen to him. For it is better to listen to Christian teaching from a man who is circumcised, than to Judaism from one who is not. But if neither speaks about Jesus Christ, I hold them pillars and tombs of the dead, bearing only the names of the dead." Ignatius is facing a strong Judaizing movement which wanted to observe the Sabbath instead of Sunday, revered the High Priest to the point of forgetting the pre-eminence due to Jesus Christ, and tended to put the O.T. above the gospel (Magn. 9.1; Philad. 9.1f; 8.2).[2] The members

---

[1] *Beginnings*, iv.271, states that "by the second century this question was almost dead, but when Luke wrote it obviously was important, at least in Jerusalem. Was it elsewhere? Probably not after 70." But no evidence is produced.

[2] See discussion in W. Bauer, *Hdb.z.N.T.* (Tübingen, 1920), 239f.

of this movement seem, from the passage quoted, to be Gentiles who are not circumcised and do not ask for circumcision.[1] What is important for our question is that, even though Ignatius is opposing these Judaizers so strongly, he yet continues to recognize that there are Jewish Christians who have a right to exist. It seems that the ingredients of the situation we have seen presupposed in Acts are already being assembled. The extent to which Gentile Christians should observe the Jewish cultic practices is a live question, although the Judaizers in this case are not asking for circumcision, and there still exist groups of Jewish Christians who have continued to circumcise their children and who are tolerated by the dominant Gentile part of the Church.

In Justin's Dialogue with Trypho we find a much closer parallel to Acts, particularly in chapter 47.[2]

Trypho asked whether a man who had acknowledged that Jesus was the Messiah and trusted in him, but still wished to observe the Mosaic Law, would be saved.

Justin replied, "In my opinion, Trypho, such a man would be saved, but only as long as he did not try to persuade others— I mean Gentiles who have been cut off from error through the Messiah—to observe the things he observed. That is, he must not tell them that they will only be saved if they observe these things. . . ."

Trypho: "Why did you say, 'In my opinion such a man will be saved'? There must be some who deny that these people will be saved."

"There are," I replied, "and they refuse to engage them in conversation or invite them into their homes, but I do not agree with them. It is because of a weakness in understanding that the Jewish Christians want to keep as much of the Law of

---

[1] See J. B. Lightfoot, *Apostolic Fathers*, Pt. 2, sect. 1 (London, 1885), 263f.

[2] The similarity was first pointed out by Schwegler (1846); see *Beginnings*, ii.374 n 2. See also the articles by A. Ritschl and F. Overbeck already cited. The fullest discussion of Justin's evidence (without, however, mention of the possible relationship to Acts) is by A. Harnack, *Judentum und Judenchristentum in Justins Dialog mit Trypho*, *T.U.*, iii.9 (=39. Band) (Leipzig, 1913), 47–92.

Moses as is possible under the present circumstances;[1] we know that it was imposed because of the hard-heartedness of the people. However, if they wish to go on holding to it alongside of their hope concerning this Messiah and the natural and supernatural moral and religious demands, and as long as they choose to live with Christians and the faithful without, as I have said, urging them to be circumcised like them or to keep the Sabbath or to do anything else they observe, then I maintain that they should be received into our fellowship and treated like kinsmen and brothers."

"But if, Trypho," I continued, "these compatriots of yours who claim to believe in this Messiah compel Gentiles who have likewise believed to live in all respects by the Mosaic Law and will not otherwise associate with them, I too will not recognize them."

"Those they succeed in persuading to submit to the observance of the Law while continuing to confess God's Messiah may perhaps, in my opinion, be saved. But those who had once confessed and recognized that this man (Jesus) was the Messiah and, for whatever reason, have gone over to the observance of the Law and have denied that he was the Messiah will, in my opinion, have no chance of salvation unless they change their minds before they die."

This extract shows again that the problem of the extent to which one should keep the Law of Moses was still alive. Some Gentile Christians were being persuaded to join the Jewish Christians in following the full range of Mosaic practices, and some were even going so far as to apostatize completely to Judaism. Justin firmly condemns any Jewish Christians who encourage Gentile Christians to observe the Law, but he adopts a tolerant attitude to Jewish Christians who are content to live with the rest of the Church without frightening their fellow Christians with the prospect of losing salvation for not keeping the Law. Justin admits that other Gentile Christians are not as tolerant as he is; they deny that the Jewish Christians who

---

[1] In chap. 46 Trypho has admitted that it is now impossible to perform the Mosaic sacrifices, because there is no Temple.

continue to observe the Law are Christians at all. As Harnack has pointed out, Justin would scarcely have admitted that the other view existed if his own view had not been in the minority, or at least under heavy fire.[1] This, however, is almost the only difference one can detect between Justin's position and Luke's, and it may be accounted for by the fact that the unsuccessful Bar Cochba revolt has occurred between Luke's time and Justin's.[2] The *modus vivendi* which was established in Luke's time, or which he believed should have been established, may well have been challenged when the Jewish people fell into deeper disgrace after the revolt had failed. The arrangement was otherwise the same as the one Justin was advocating. Attempts from the Jewish Christian side to impose the Law of Moses are as firmly squashed in Acts as in Justin. On the other hand, the right of the Jewish Christians to continue the observance of the Mosaic Law, as far as one could (Acts 15.10), was fully and freely granted by Paul himself who, as a Jew, never deviated from its observance (Acts 25.8 etc.).

It has been argued in Chapter One that Justin had not seen Luke-Acts. Even if he had, the agreement with Luke on this issue could scarely be due to Justin's copying Acts, since both Trypho and Christian readers of the Dialogue would know if the situation he presented did not correspond to conditions at the time. Nor should it be forgotten that Justin never once mentions Paul's name, here or anywhere else.[3] The close agreement between Acts and Justin's Dialogue on this question of the status of Jewish Christians within the Church is one of the most compelling arguments in favour of the second-century date for Acts.

Finally, there is a great deal of second-century evidence that the so-called Apostolic Decree (or rather, the terms it contained) was important in the whole discussion. Justin denounces before Trypho those Christians who eat meat offered to idols (Dial. 35). When Trypho introduces the matter, Justin

[1] Op. cit., 86 and n.
[2] Overbeck, op. cit., 337f, adds that in Acts the observance of the Law is obligatory for Jewish Christians and in Justin, optional.
[3] See 25-8 above.

states that this was the chief way to distinguish those heretics who, in one way or another, denied the Creator and abandoned the O.T.: Marcians,[1] Valentinians, Basilidians, Saturnilians, and so on. It seems that the prohibition against eating meat offered to idols is a mark by which the orthodox are distinguished from the gnostic heretics; the fact that it is Trypho who first raised the matter in the Dialogue suggests that this test might have been made decisive at the insistence of the Jewish communities within the Church.

In Rev. 2.14,20, eating food offered to idols and committing adultery are condemned by the Seer. In both cases the O.T. context, the stories of Balaam and Jezebel, shows that a general relapse into heathenism is being indicated; it remains significant, however, that it is these two practical matters, and no others, which are singled out on the basis of the O.T. narrative.

There is a great deal of evidence from the second half of the second century that the remaining parts of the Decree were in force in some parts of the Church.[2] Twice Christians are recorded as defending themselves against the charge that they eat children by saying that they did not even eat meat with the blood in it (Minucius Felix 36.6; Biblis in Eus., *H.E.*, v.1.26), and Tertullian provides fuller information when he says that Christians did not eat the blood of animals, and therefore abstained from eating animals that had been strangled or had died naturally (Apol. 9.13). The Syriac version of the Apology of Aristides 15 also states that Christians "do not eat of the meats of idol sacrifices".[3]

Finally, the Pseudo-Clementine literature shows that the prohibitions against eating food offered to idols and against eating blood and strangled animals were combined by this Jewish Christian group.[4] Rec. iv.36 lists three types of sins which pollute the marriage garment of a Christian, that is, his

---

[1] Marcionites?

[2] Haenchen, op. cit., 418f.

[3] Tr. by J. Rendel Harris, *Texts and Studies*, i (Cambridge, 1891), 49.

[4] Einar Molland, "La circoncision, le baptême et l'autorité du décret apostolique (Actes 15.28 sq.) dans les milieux judéo-chrétiens des Pseudo-Clémentines", *Studia Theologica*, ix (Lund, 1956), 1–39.

baptism.[1] "Those which pollute both soul and body are these: partaking of the table of demons (that is, eating sacrifices), or of blood, or of a dead animal which has been strangled, or of anything else which has been offered to demons" (cf. Hom. viii.23; vii.4). On the basis of the fact that Hom. vii.4 adds to this list a command to wash after pollution, which probably refers to washing after menstruation or sexual intercourse, together with a form of the Golden Rule, Molland jumps to the conclusion that this command about washing is what was meant by πορνεία in the Decree in Acts.[2] The conclusion by no means follows. There is no instance of πορνεία being given this meaning, and washing after intercourse is both a common Jewish requirement (cf. Justin, Dial. 46.2) and part of the extensive system of ablutions practised by the people responsible for the Pseudo-Clementines. The Pseudo-Clementines do not provide evidence that some Christians preserved the Apostolic Decree independently of Acts,[3] but simply that the prohibition against eating food offered to idols, and blood, and strangled animals was current among some Jewish Christians in the second century.

The surprising conclusion is that nowhere in early Christian literature, apart from Acts, do we find all four clauses of the Decree mentioned together. If the practice of abstaining from eating food offered to idols and from eating blood and strangled animals was based on an actual Decree which the Jerusalem Church had promulgated in the primitive period, we should expect that those who advocated this practice would appeal to Apostolic authority. We should probably also expect πορνεία to be mentioned more often in this context. The fact that neither of these expectations is fulfilled makes it very unlikely, particularly in view of Paul's ignorance of such a Decree, that it goes back to apostolic times. It is far more likely that Luke discovered the terms of the Decree in an old source, and that they represented a specific Jewish Christian proposal that Gentile

---

[1] This is a gnostic idea; G. Strecker, *Das Judenchristentum in den Pseudoklementinen*, *T.U.*, v.15 (= 70. Band) (Berlin, 1958), 203.

[2] Op. cit., 28.  [3] Ibid., 28 and 39.

Christians should observe the Levitical requirements for "strangers within the gate".[1] Luke would by no means have accepted the assumption that Gentile Christians should regard themselves as guests in Israel of the Jewish Christians, but he probably did understand that the practices mentioned in the Decree were acceptable to Jewish Christians, and that they were already used to distinguish orthodox Gentile believers from the unorthodox who were sliding into gnosticism. He embodied the Decree in his text because it seemed to justify the customs already observed in the Church, and seemed to help buttress the tolerant relationship which he wished to see existing between Jewish and Gentile Christians. The Decree may be old, but it is unlikely that it had apostolic authority; the way it is used in Acts shows that it is designed to seal a compact which the Gentile Church in the first half of the second century might have concluded with the Jewish brethren. A few years later Justin's Dialogue with Trypho shows that the supporters of this arrangement were already on the defensive, and the organized Jewish Christian churches seem to have disappeared by the end of the century. Acts had used Paul's name to support the Agreement, but the subsequent publication of Paul's letters and the Marcionite controversy seem to have helped to put an end to practical compromises over the observance of the Law. The position represented by the writer of Acts only existed for a time.

The theology of Acts on this question, as on the larger question of the relationship between the Church and the Jews, is a practical and historical theology. None of the theoretical arguments which Paul employed are invoked. The history of the apostolic age has been reconstructed out of the scanty material available in order to demonstrate that a workable arrangement was possible between Jews and Gentiles in the Church. It is out of the question that Gentiles should be circumcised and become full Jews, since the work of the Spirit in the strong and living Gentile Church has shown that to be unnecessary, but there are some Mosaic cultic regulations which

[1] Ritschl, op. cit., 301f.

would preserve the distinctive connection with the O.T. (for the moral requirements of the O.T. can be found elsewhere, in the sayings of Jesus and the common moral instinct of mankind), and these practices are already widely observed in the Church. Luke has used the history of Paul's visits to Jerusalem, which he knows were of great importance in the early days of the reception of Gentile Christians, to show Christians in his own day how they should settle their problem of the relations between Jewish and Gentile Christians. We should not be surprised that his work reflects the situation in the first half of the second century better than it portrays the events in the life of the primitive Church.

CHAPTER FIVE

# THE TITLES GIVEN TO JESUS

THE LAST two chapters have explored the theological attitude
which Luke took to the Jews and the Jewish Christians. The
chief contention was that Luke was a theologian who believed
that God had revealed his solution to the theological decisions
facing the contemporary Church in the history of the primitive
Church. He believed that God had used the rebelliousness of
the Jews to drive the Church out into the Gentile world, and
that it should boldly accept its destiny and try to capture the
Roman empire for the faith, as he was himself attempting by
writing Luke-Acts; he also believed that the practice of the
early Church provided a model for the relationship which
should exist between Jewish and Gentile Christians in his day.
But to say this is not to deny that Luke was a historian. We have
seen again and again that he made full use of the source material
which was available. He may have misjudged its antiquity,
and he may have been unable to avoid anachronism, but he
believed that his account of the events was historical and not
fictitious. But if the proper analogy for Acts is not *Gulliver's
Travels*, a fictitious history with a moral, neither is it the chapters
on the history of Christianity in the *Cambridge Ancient History*.
The proper analogy is something like Marx's history of the
1830 revolution in France, *The Eighteenth Brumaire of Louis
Bonaparte*, which is certainly history, but is also propaganda.
In the course of his analysis, Marx preached the historical
dynamic of the class struggle. He presented the class struggle as
the key not only to the history of that revolution but also as the
key to the coming universal revolution, and indeed to the whole
course of human history.

This type of history, which is designed to draw lessons from history and to win men's allegiance to a cause, poses a problem for later generations who wish to obtain an objective view of what happened. Like Luke, Christians to-day believe that the practice and beliefs of the primitive Church are extremely important for their own Church life. They naturally want to go behind Luke's interpretation and to extract evidence for primitive practice on which they, in turn, can build their own theology. They may become impatient at attempts to uncover the Lucan theology, and prefer to turn to the more important task of finding out what the first Apostles taught and the first Christians believed. This is not a hopeless historical quest, but one aim of the present chapter is to show that it is all too easy to arrive at false conclusions if the theological purpose and the theological background of Luke are not taken into account at every step. It is necessary to keep in mind the theology of Acts in the historical setting of church life in the early second century while searching for the theology of the primitive Church.

The titles by which Jesus is called have been chosen for this study because the claim is most often made that here Luke has preserved primitive usage. Although some recognition is given by supporters of this theory to Luke's own theological position—few scholars would deny that he at least sometimes expressed his own point of view—a sharp distinction is drawn between that and the theology of the early Church which he incorporated into the narrative. For example, a recent examination of Peter's speech at Pentecost concludes that "here . . . one finds specific expressions and ideas, in particular a Jewish Christian conception of the Messiah and the gospel, which would be completely foreign to Luke as a Hellenist, but which were most likely characteristic of Peter and the primitive Church".[1] This view presupposes that Luke possessed verbal records of what the Apostles preached, and that he inserted them into his story though the language and ideas were neither current in his own Church nor really comprehensible to him.

[1] Bo Reicke, *Glaube und Leben der Urgemeinde* (Zürich, 1957), 40; cf. a similar argument, 46, 50 and *passim*.

The evidence to which we must now turn suggests, on the contrary, that Luke possessed no connected apostolic sermons, and that, when he employed primitive terms, they had been almost completely assimilated into his theology. This does not mean that Acts is valueless as a source for primitive Christological titles, but rather that they will not be discovered by creating a rigid picture of Luke's theology and asserting that everything which is incompatible with that picture is primitive. Luke's theology is catholic; it represents a confluence of many streams of thought, some joining the river near its source, and some flowing in lower down, but by Luke's time they are almost completely mingled.[1]

The two major titles for Jesus in Acts are χριστός and κύριος. In both cases Luke occasionally uses them in a purely primitive way, but in both cases his usage is dominated by the theology of his time. He employs the titles primarily to further two ends: to establish that the O.T. is a Christian and not a Jewish book, and to demonstrate that Jesus alone meets the requirements of the messianic doctrine contained in it. As far as we can tell, neither of these dominated the primitive usage of the terms.

As Cadbury has pointed out, there are three peculiarities of the Lucan usage of χριστός: it is used very rarely as a name; it is never used by itself as a name (or, more precisely, as the equivalent of a name, like "Der Führer" in twentieth-century Germany, or "The Lord Protector" in seventeenth-century England); and finally, it usually bears the full meaning, "The Messiah".[2] All three are true also for Luke's Gospel.

The only cases where χριστός is used as a name are in combination with "Jesus". "Jesus Christ", used as a name in the way with which we are familiar to-day, is found in eight places: 2.38 (the appeal to be baptized at the end of the Pentecost speech); 3.6 (the formula used to heal the lame beggar); 4.10 (a repetition of the previous formula); 10.36 (the opening

---

[1] See now Ulrich Wilckens, *Die Missionsreden der Apg., Form- und Traditionsgeschichtliche Untersuchungen* (Neukirchen Kreis Moers, 1961), esp. 155–78.

[2] *Beginnings*, v.357–9.

of Peter's sermon to Cornelius); 10.48 (the formula used in baptizing Cornelius and his friends); 11.17 (Peter's report that they had believed and been baptized); 15.26 (the credentials of Barnabas and Paul contained in the letter sent out from Jerusalem); and 16.18 (the formula used by Paul to exorcize the girl with an oracular spirit).[1] It seems that the phrase was one reserved for solemn occasions—preaching, baptizing, exorcizing, commending emissaries—and not one to be used outside of direct speech. We are not in a position to explain this yet, but the alternative explanations would seem to be either that this is the primitive usage, confined to the Palestinian Church before Paul made it well known and used in Gentile circles,[2] or that it is by Luke's time an archaic expression, only employed on solemn ecclesiastical occasions.

Apart from these cases, Luke's usage consistently demands that χριστός should be translated "Messiah". It usually has the article; it is always used when Jews, or men familiar with Jewish customs, are being addressed; and it is often used where the identification of the Messiah is the point of the argument. The last point may be illustrated by quoting the report of what Paul said in Thessalonica: "For three Sabbaths he conducted discussions with them on the basis of the Scriptures, explaining and demonstrating that the Messiah had to suffer and rise from the dead, and that 'this is the Messiah, Jesus whom I proclaim to you'" (17.2f).[3] The same argument, that only Jesus fulfils the requirements set down for the O.T. Messiah, appears in the context in which the word is used at 2.31,36; 3.18,20; 4.26; probably 5.42; 8.5; 9.22,34 (reading Ἰησοῦς ὁ χριστός with AE etc.); 18.5,28; and 26.23. There is a curious phrase in

---

[1] The evidence for omitting χριστός in 28.31 is ℵ* *614* and a number of other minuscules, syr^h, and should probably be accepted. The evidence for omission in five of the cases cited in the text is too slight to be accepted: 2.38 (Iren. syr^pesh); 3.6; 4.10; 16.18 (all sah^B); 10.48 (HLPS5).

[2] C. Ryder Smith, "The Names 'Christ' and 'Jesus' in the Acts", *E.T.*, xix (1907–8), 45f: ". . . the writer of Acts was a *Gentile* Christian of *so early a period* that in his time . . . the combination 'Jesus Christ' was not yet taken over by the Gentile Churches, though it was common among Jewish Christians."

[3] See note in *Beginnings*, iv.205.

24.24 where the reading is disputed. B ℵ 81 etc., read τῆς εἰς χριστὸν Ἰησοῦν πίστεως, but ℵᶜ A Cᵛⁱᵈ H P syrᵖᵉˢʰ sah(1) 5 omit Ιησουν. If the Vaticanus reading is correct, this would be the only case of the phrase "Christ Jesus" in Luke-Acts. (The parallel with Acts 3.20; 5.42; 18.5,28 is illusory; the article before χριστός in each of these cases shows that the two words do not go together to form a name, and that the correct translation is "the Messiah, Jesus". The forms χριστὸς κύριος (Luke 2.11) and χριστὸν βασιλέα (Luke 23.2) are correlative titles, and do not affect this argument.) That, and the fact that a scribe would be more likely to add "Jesus" than to omit it, show that the Vaticanus reading is probably to be rejected. When this excision is made, we are left with an interesting scene. Felix and his Jewish wife Drusilla summon Paul to hear his version of messianic belief. Paul's discourse consists, as we shall try to show in Chapter Six, of a typical Jewish apologetical statement. The Christian reader would of course know that Paul could hardly speak about the judgement to come without mentioning the Judge, but Luke's point is that Christianity can be understood and proclaimed as Jewish messianic doctrine. He thus reinforces the argument which Paul had already used in open court, that he was a perfectly orthodox Jew who had found in Jesus the only fulfilment of orthodox Jewish messianic expectation.

It has been argued that this use of χριστός as a Jewish title meaning "The Messiah" is a sign of primitive usage, reflecting the period before the word became almost a name for Jesus.[1] A contrast is made with Pauline usage, and the contrast is certainly striking. Paul often uses χριστός by itself as the nearest thing to a name, and it is rare to find him using it in a context where "Messiah" is definitely the required translation. The closest he comes to this is when he says "we preach Christ crucified χριστὸν ἐσταυρωμένον" (1 Cor. 1.23), and when he includes "Christ according to the flesh ὁ χριστὸς τὸ κατὰ σάρκα" in the list of the possessions of the Jews (Rom. 9.5).

---

[1] Harnack, cit. *Beginnings,* v.358; C. Ryder Smith, op. cit.

Luke's usage consistently implies that χριστός was a Jewish title with a fixed and definite meaning, and that it was possible to conduct an argument with Jews as to whether Jesus did or did not meet the specified requirements. Paul's usage, on the other hand, is much less definite; in the passage quoted from I Corinthians he is merely saying that the Jews were scandalized at the idea of a crucified Messiah, not that Jesus failed to measure up to an agreed Jewish picture. Paul's usage perhaps corresponds to the way the title "Der Führer" was used in Nazi Germany. Many people in Germany in the 'twenties were looking for a Leader, but there was no agreed picture of what he should be like.[1] When Hitler appeared, the title was applied to him and was used almost like a name. When one said "Der Führer", no one doubted that Hitler, and Hitler alone, was meant. Of course this analogy is not exact enough to explain the subtleties of Paul's usage, but it does show the contrast between Paul and Luke. In Luke we have to do with a disputable category of messiahship; in Paul with a vaguely longed for Anointed One who has suddenly come to life in Jesus.

If the distinction made here is a valid one, it is no longer possible to explain the difference between Luke and Paul on the assumption that Luke reflects the more primitive state of affairs. The true explanation is perhaps suggested by the investigations of G. F. Moore, which the Editors of *The Beginnings of Christianity* sum up in these words: "The point in the previous discussion most important for the investigation of early Christianity is that 'Messiah' is essentially an adjective meaning consecrated or appointed by God, and was not the prerogative title of any single person until later than the time of Christ."[2] Moore explains that, although there were widespread expectations that "a divinely appointed head of the people should one day appear, with whom better days would come", for whom "the anointed (king)" was a popular name, it was not until after A.D. 70 that Messianic prophecy assumed an engrossing impor-

[1] See the letter of G. Kittel to Karl Barth, 15 June 1934, *Ein theologischer Briefwechsel* (Stüttgart, 1934), 12.

[2] *Beginnings*, i.362; Moore's discussion, 346–62.

tance, and engaged the attention of the rabbis.[1] Luke's use of the
term χριστός implies that discussions with Jews about the positive qualities of the Messiah had been held, and they could
hardly have taken such an explicit form before the Jewish
religious leaders had begun to formulate a coherent messianic
doctrine. If Moore is right, that did not happen until after
A.D. 70.

The evidence of the Apostolic Fathers and the Apologists
supports the view that the Lucan use of χριστός is late rather
than early. By far the most common use of "Christ" in the
Apostolic Fathers is in the formula "Jesus Christ" (rarely
"Christ Jesus"); "Christ" is frequently used by itself as a
name, particularly in 1 and 2 Clement; but χριστός very rarely
requires to be translated by "The Messiah". The only clear
examples of the need to translate in this way occur in 1 Clem.
17.1, the messianic prophecy isolated by Professor Kilpatrick,
and Barn. 12.10f, a reference to the synoptic discussion of
Psalm 110.[2] This seems to accord very closely with the Pauline
usage. When we come to Justin Martyr's Dialogue with
Trypho we encounter, for the first time, χριστός used frequently
to denote the abstract category of Messiah, though it should be
noted that the word is also used by itself in the Apology as a
name. It is probable, then, that the peculiarities of the Lucan
use of "Christ" should be explained against a background of
Christian and Jewish disputes in the second century about the
identity of the Messiah. This sort of dispute, involving proof
and counter-proof from O.T. Scripture, was probably inconceivable any earlier. Before the rabbis evolved a positive
messianic doctrine it was difficult to argue except in negatives:
the Anointed One will not be (merely) David's son, or the
Anointed One will not be crucified, but, when messianic
doctrine has become a central concern in Jewish thought and
the Messiah a fixed category, the Dialogue with Trypho and
Lucan use of χριστός become possible.

[1] Ibid., i.356, 359f.
[2] Perhaps also 1 Clem. 41.1,2; Ign. Eph. 18.2; Rom. 7.3, v.l.; Mar. Pol.
14.2.

To point out this peculiarity of Lucan usage is not to deny, however, that he can still use the term to represent primitive theological ideas. If it is possible to discover in Acts traces of a Christology which differs from the dominant Christology, it might be arguable that Luke was employing a source and preserving a primitive messianic doctrine.

Dr J. A. T. Robinson has argued that not one, but two, incompatible Christologies are embedded in the first few chapters of Acts.[1] The first, in Acts 2, represents "what was to become the accepted thesis of the early Church, that, by virtue of his resurrection to the right hand of God, Jesus is 'both Lord and Christ'".[2] The second, in Acts 3 (and also in Acts 7), precedes, logically at least, the recognition of the importance of the resurrection, and states that, while Jesus has already appeared, the Messiah is still to come—and he will be Jesus. Both these Christologies, it is argued, are earlier than Luke's own Christology, in which the use of the title "Christ" for Jesus is pushed right back to his birth.

The crowning statement of Peter's Pentecost sermon in Acts 2 almost certainly implies that the death, resurrection, and ascension mark the point where God made Jesus both Lord and Messiah, just as earlier in the speech Jesus is said to have received the promise of the Holy Spirit from the Father when he ascended. Both doctrines seem to contradict the belief that Jesus was always Christ and always possessed the Holy Spirit. "The statements with which the speech for the time being ends are derived from older traditions, and use formulae which do not correspond to Lucan Christology. Luke assumes that Jesus had already possessed both the Spirit and his status as Son of God during his earthly life (cf. Luke 2.40ff; 3.22; 4.18; 9.35)" (Haenchen).[3] We should also add, to complete the picture, that Paul asserts that the words from Psalm 2, "You

---

[1] "The Most Primitive Christology of All?", *J. T.S.*, N.S., vii (1956) 177–88; *Jesus and his Coming, the Emergence of a Doctrine* (London, 1957), chap. 7.

[2] Op. cit., *J.T.S.* (1956), 180.

[3] Op. cit., 155.

are my son; to-day have I begotten you", are spoken at Jesus'
resurrection (Acts 13.33). It would be fruitless to deny that
some sort of a contradiction is involved here; what is important
to see is that Luke shows signs of being perfectly aware of the
contradiction, and expounds a theology designed to contain the
differences.

A great deal is rightly made of the "messianic secret" in
St Mark's Gospel, but it is often overlooked that St Luke also
has inherited a doctrine of messianic reticence, which he applies
even more rigidly, in some ways, than Mark. In Mark Jesus
once, and only once, broke his silence about his own status,
at the climax to his appearance before the Sanhedrin. When he
was asked, "Are you the Messiah, the son of the Blessed?" he
answered with a decisive, "I am" (Mark 14.61f). Luke, who
shows no sign of employing a special source at this point,
altered this to ὑμεῖς λέγετε ὅτι ἐγώ εἰμι, probably on the
model of the later answer to Pilate (Mark 15.2; Luke 23.3),
thus preserving the dogma that Jesus did not openly claim his
messiahship until his foreordained course was run and he was
risen from the dead. It is true that in Luke the Angels proclaimed his messiahship, Simeon recognized it, and the demons
acknowledged it, but these represent the angelic, prophetic, and
demonic foreknowledge of what God had ordained (2.11,26;
4.41). When the people, their leaders, and the thief on the cross
called Jesus "Messiah" they were only taunting him with the
absurdity of the idea that the Messiah could allow himself to be
crucified without escaping (23.2,35,39). When Peter confessed
that the Lord was "the Anointed of God" the disciples were
sternly commanded—more sternly and more specifically than
in Mark—"to repeat this to no one" (9.21; cf. Mark 8.30).
Only on the road to Emmaus, when the disciples had despaired
of ever seeing again "him who was going to redeem Israel",
did Jesus claim the title of "Messiah". He could not be called
"Messiah" until he was known to be the suffering Messiah
(24.13–35, espec. 21,26,30,31).

Luke seems to have taken the doctrine that God first made
Jesus Messiah and Lord after the resurrection, and worked it

into his total theology by insisting that not until Jesus had suffered and risen from the dead did he fulfil the messianic prophecies. In Acts, as we have seen, Christian preaching to the Jews concentrated on making the same point, that only one who had suffered and been raised from the dead could be called "Messiah". When Jesus was called "Messiah" before his crucifixion, that was only by virtue of a prophetic foreknowledge of what God was going to perform, and was comparable to O.T. prophecy of the same event.

The seeming contradiction between the fact that Jesus from the beginning of his ministry was anointed with the Spirit,[1] and the statement in Peter's speech at Pentecost that he received the Spirit when he ascended is easier to resolve. Although Jesus himself was anointed with the Spirit from the beginning of his work, he did not receive the Spirit to "pour out" on those who had come to believe in him until after he had ascended into heaven. God had given him the Spirit to enable him to accomplish his divinely ordained work, but only when he was made Messiah did he have the power to give the promised gift to all believers.

The belief that Jesus was made Messiah at his resurrection is a primitive one, but it is also a continuing tradition. The earliest witness to the idea is probably Phil. 2.6–11, a hymn quoted by Paul from an older source. In it Jesus was first given the "name which is above every name" because of his obedience to death. The messiahship of Jesus is not particularly in question here, and probably did not appear in the document Paul was quoting (χριστός is omitted in verse 11 by G *1898* Or Eus Hil Ambst), but the general tenor clearly corresponds to the idea we are tracing. Jesus put aside his heavenly status to take the form of a servant, but he was not given the highest name until he had died on the cross and been exalted. St Matthew's Gospel, however, shows that the idea was kept alive in Church tradition, despite the natural tendency to say that

---

[1] It is not necessary to suppose that the use of the verb χρίω in the citation from Isaiah in Luke 4.18 implies that Jesus here openly claimed to be Messiah.

Jesus had always been "Christ". Like Luke, he also changed the unequivocal "I am", spoken by Jesus at his trial according to Mark, into συ εἶπας, a change which was made independently of Luke (Matt. 26.64; Mark 14.62). The way Jesus' final commission to his disciples was phrased, "All power has been given to me (ἐδόθη)", seems to imply that he had just received his power at the resurrection. The unequivocal welcoming of Peter's confession at Caesarea Philippi does not substantially alter the picture, since Matthew is careful to state that Peter's words were the direct result of divine revelation, and that Peter himself would not become the foundation-stone of the Church which lives by this confession until Jesus' death and resurrection had intervened. Matthew, too, has consciously incorporated the idea that Jesus became Messiah at the resurrection into his theology.

Perhaps Luke is not quite successful in reconciling the two ideas, that Jesus was always Messiah and that he only became Messiah after his resurrection, but the evidence suggests that he was conscious of the difficulty and had tried to evolve a catholic theology which would do justice to both strands. He had inherited an ancient tradition, but the evidence from Matthew shows that it was not something lying forgotten in a primitive source, which he alone had discovered. It was still a living part of the Church's theology about the time he wrote.

Dr Robinson finds a second distinct Christology in Acts 3.12–26: Jesus was not Messiah during his ministry, but was yet to return in that capacity. The argument that this was the original meaning of Peter's words depends on two assumptions, first, that the titles applied to Jesus earlier in the speech, particularly τὸν παῖδα αὐτοῦ and προφήτην (3.13,22), were premessianic titles, and second, that the phrase "his Messiah should suffer" (3.18) was an interpolation of a purely Lucan idea into the original source. On the first assumption it should be noted that Jesus is also called τὸν ἅγιον καὶ δίκαιον and τὸν ἀρχηγὸν τῆς ζωῆς. These terms can scarcely be called premessianic; a comparison of Luke 4.34 and 41 shows that ὁ ἅγιος is messianic, as ὁ δίκαιος in Acts 7.52 also seems to be.

We have to discuss the παῖς phrase later, but our conclusion then will be that it is a fully messianic term. Of course these conclusions all concern the meaning Luke gave to the words; it is still possible that he had radically misinterpreted an underlying source which bore the meaning Dr Robinson ascribes to the passage. His second assumption, that the phrase about the suffering Messiah is a Lucan insertion, cannot be tested until we know whether the context is non-Lucan. The idea of a suffering Messiah is certainly Lucan, or rather, since it is also found in Justin Martyr, it is the doctrine of Luke's Church, but whether it was interpolated depends on whether the rest of the speech as a whole came from an early source.

Finally, it may be doubted whether even the underlying source expounds the doctrine Dr Robinson reads out of it, that the Jews should seize the opportunity for repentance which was still open, "that the age of renewal may dawn and God may be able to send Jesus, *this time* as their appointed Messiah".[1] The actual words in verses 19 to 21 do not state that Jesus will come for the first time as Messiah when the Jews repent, and the word δέξασθαι may even imply the opposite: "Repent and return for the obliteration of your sins, so that times of rest (or refreshment) from the presence of the Lord may come, and he may send your ordained Messiah Jesus, whom heaven must receive until the times of the restoration of all the things of which God spoke by the mouth of his holy prophets from the first." Again we must suspend judgement, since the idea which Dr Robinson discovers behind Luke's words may well correspond to a primitive understanding of the relationship between Jesus' earthly status and his future status; it may be, for example, that "the Son of Man" was at first purely a future title which was later applied to Jesus in his earthly ministry.[2] Luke may be passing on primitive material. When we examine in more detail the other titles in this speech, however, it will become clear that they have such varied antecedents that it is unlikely that

---

[1] Op. cit., *J.T.S.*, (1956), 181, my italics.
[2] Heinz Eduard Tödt, *Der Menschensohn in der synoptischen Überlieferung* (Gütersloh, 1959).

the speech as a whole existed in one source. It is more likely that Luke constructed it from a number of different elements, some new and some old. He has designed the speech to fit perfectly into the developing pattern of Acts.[1]

Although Luke has taken up traditional messianic ideas, he generally used the title χριστός as an abstract and well-defined category, that is, in a sense which had developed later in Christian thought. The meaning given to the term and the contexts in which it appears provide clues for a fuller understanding of the theology of Acts and the theology of the Church for which Acts was written; it is much more difficult to use this evidence in discovering the Christology of the primitive Church.

The title κύριος for Jesus originated in the Aramaic-speaking Church. "Marana tha", 1 Cor. 16.22; Did. 10.6; cf. Rev. 22.20, was an Aramaic prayer to Jesus[2] and, as Burkitt has pointed out, this liturgical form is the Achilles' heel of all theories which derive the title κύριος from Hellenistic religious practice.[3] The way the title is used in Acts, however, shows that the author was writing when the Aramaic origins had long been forgotten. Two distinct influences have been at work, as we shall see by noting the way in which the title is used for both God and Jesus, and by examining the story of Paul's encounter with Jesus on the Damascus road.

Luke again shows that he is drawing on old traditions when he has Peter's Pentecost speech end with a quotation from the opening words of Psalm 110. It is very likely that this Psalm was long pondered by the Aramaic-speaking Church which prayed to Jesus, "Marana tha". This appears from the fact that Paul's theology, especially as expressed in Rom. 1.3f, seems to

---

[1] Dr Robinson's argument, *Jesus and His Coming*, 144 and note, that it is impossible to imagine this appeal to the Jews to repent being made in A.D. 90, i.e., that the speech must be primitive, fails to take account of Luke's purpose. Luke wished to show that, though the Jews were given every opportunity to repent, they still refused, and therefore the gospel was taken to the Gentiles. He made the speech fit the historical circumstances; see Chapter Three above.

[2] Against Bultmann, *Theology of the N.T.*, i (Eng. tr., London, 1952), 51f.

[3] F. C. Burkitt, *Christian Beginnings* (London, 1924), 49ff.

imply a knowledge of the argument employed by Jesus on the basis of Psalm 110 (Mark 12.35–7 and parallels). The use of Psalm 110 by Jesus cannot have been designed to deny outright that the Messiah was of the seed of David, for that would have meant ignoring a host of other O.T. messianic passages.[1] It must, then, have been an attempt to prove that much more should also be claimed for the Messiah than simply that he was of the seed of David; the Messiah should also be called Lord.[2] Paul appears to be quoting from a formulation of this doctrine in the opening verses of Romans, where he wrote about the two "natures" of Christ, of the seed of David according to the flesh, Son of God in power according to the Holy Spirit.[3] He may have been aware of the connection between that doctrine and Psalm 110, for he often returned to the Psalm when speaking about Christ's exalted position (1 Cor. 15.25; Col. 3.1; Rom. 8.34; cf. Eph. 1.10). But the Aramaic-speaking Church read the O.T. in Hebrew and would be fully aware of the distinction in Psalm 110 between "the Lord" יהוה and "my Lord" אֲדֹנִי. Paul shows such an awareness by avoiding for the most part using κύριος for God, and he always did so when citing this Psalm. The formula with which he began three of his letters may be taken as typical of the usage of the Church at his time:

> Grace to you and peace
> from God our Father
> and the Lord Jesus Christ.
> (Rom. 1.7; 1 Cor. 1.3; 2 Cor. 1.2; cf. Eph. 1.2)

"Lord" was almost completely confined to Jesus, and God was called "Father".[4]

In the purely Greek-speaking Church, which had no scriptures apart from the LXX, it would be impossible for long to

---

[1] E. Lohmeyer, *Markus* (11th ed., Göttingen, 1957), 262.

[2] G. Bornkamm, *Jesus von Nazareth* (Stuttgart, 1956), 206.

[3] There is evidence that it was not Paul's own formulation. These verses contain two phrases and one word never found elsewhere in Paul's writings: διὰ τῶν προφητῶν and ἐν γραφαῖς ἁγίαις (v. 2), and ὁρίζω (v. 4).

[4] E. Lohmeyer, *Probleme paulinischer Theologie* (Darmstadt, 1954), "Briefliche Grussüberschriften", 9–29, esp. 28.

follow that part of the Church which read the Scriptures in Hebrew in avoiding the use of κύριος for God the Father. Luke applied this title to God almost as often as he did to Jesus, and when Psalm 110.1 was quoted in Heb. 8.1 the writer went on in the next verse to call God ὁ κύριος. At this stage there are no indications that there was any confusion between the two Lords, or any attempt to claim divinity for Jesus because he was called Lord.[1]

The story of Paul's encounter with Jesus on the Damascus road shows another influence at work. In answer to the heavenly voice, "Saul, Saul, why do you persecute me?" he replied, "Who are you, Lord?" The dialogue raises a problem. Would the Paul we know have needed to ask who appeared to him in blinding light, speaking from heaven? From everything we can discover about Paul's background and training it must be inferred that he would never have doubted for one moment that the God of his fathers had appeared to him, if not directly as he did when the Scriptures were written, at least by his Spirit, or by means of the *Bath Qol*, or by an Angel. Why then did he ask who the Lord was? There may be a way out of the difficulty.[2] A Hebrew idiom exists which makes it possible to take Paul's counter-question not as a request for information about the identity of the visionary being, but as a request for new knowledge of the God Paul believed he was serving. In that case his use of the word "Lord" would be an acknowledgement of his belief that he was addressing the God of Israel. The appropriate Hebrew idiom occurs once in the O.T., in Ruth 3.16. Naomi greeted Ruth on her return from Boaz's thrashing floor with the words, "Who are you, my daughter?" That means perhaps "How are you, my daughter?" or, "What has happened to you, my daughter?" If Paul was familiar with this idiom, his question would have the sense, "What has become of you, Lord, when you say that my efforts to serve you are in fact your

---

[1] This is a reversal of the position expounded in my article, "The Use of ΚΥΡΙΟΣ in the Book of Acts", *Scottish Journal of Theology*, viii (1955), 155–74.
[2] Ibid.

persecution?" Unfortunately, it is almost impossible that the idiom, which occurs only once, and which is omitted by one important manuscript of the LXX (B), showing that it was becoming or had become incomprehensible to bi-lingual Jews, should provide the explanation in this case. According to Acts, Paul heard the voice and (presumably) answered in Aramaic, but in retelling the story in Greek it is very unlikely that he would have retained the primitive idiom without providing an idiomatic translation. Otherwise his audience would have gained a very misleading impression of the meaning of the dialogue.

We are forced to conclude that Paul would never have needed to ask, "Who are you, Lord?" The counter-question only has point and meaning in an environment where there are "many gods and many lords" (1 Cor. 8.5). Then one would need to know which of the heavenly beings was appearing and speaking, and one would naturally address the being from another world as "Lord".[1] Luke no more than Paul believed that the many gods and the many lords really existed, but it is possible that he or his traditional source had taken over and adapted the story of the dramatic conversion of a heathen who persecuted the Church. Stories about the conversion of men to the cult they had previously persecuted were current in the Hellenistic world, and Hellenistic Judaism has its own example, in the conversion of Heliodorus to Judaism when he was on the point of robbing the treasury in Jerusalem (2 Macc. 3).[2] Perhaps we are putting too much weight on the startled response of a man confronted with an epiphany for the first time, but it does seem most unlikely that a Jew would ask which "Lord" was speaking to him from heaven. We may, then, detect the influence of the Hellenistic environment on the story which Luke retells. It was probably in the first place a story of the

[1] Martin Werner, *Die Entstehung des christlichen Dogmas* (2nd ed., Bern and Tübingen, 1953), 309; (Eng. tr., London, 1957), 123f., argues that Paul was addressing an angel and believed that Jesus should be ranked with the angels. Did anyone believe that it was possible to persecute an angel?

[2] H. Windisch, "Die Christophanie von Damaskus und ihre religionsgeschichtlichen Parallelen", *Z.N.W.*, xxxi (1932), 1–23.

conversion of a heathen persecutor of the Church to Christianity. However, the word "Lord" has slipped past the syncretistic censorship not because that title for Jesus was governed by pagan usage, but simply because Luke was entirely accustomed to calling Jesus "Lord", and felt that it was appropriate for Paul to address him correctly. We have learnt nothing which should incline us to take pagan influence into account in plotting the developing significance of the title "Lord" as applied to Jesus, but we have found more evidence that Luke was working with material which had grown up in a pagan environment and a missionary situation.

The question whether ὁ παῖς τοῦ θεοῦ, a title given to Jesus four times in Acts 3 and 4, is an indication of the existence of a primitive Servant Christology has been hotly debated for over fifty years. The most exhaustive treatment of the question to have appeared recently is Professor Jeremias's famous article for Kittel's *Theologisches Wörterbuch zum Neuen Testament*.[1] Professor Jeremias's arguments do not seem, however, to prove his case, and we are driven to the conclusion that there was no separate "Servant Christology" which Luke might be said to have preserved.[2]

The first thing to be noticed is that the phrase ὁ παῖς τοῦ θεοῦ in the N.T. is not at all closely linked with suffering servant passages from Deutero-Isaiah. One would need very compelling evidence to prove that it was since, as Jeremias points out, it is completely anachronistic to speak of either "The Suffering Servant" or "Deutero-Isaiah". The nearest to a clear connection is found in the composite quotation from Isaiah in Matt. 12.18–21. The first part of the proof text was found by Matthew in the traditional material he was using; that part is dependent on the Hebrew text of Isa. 42.1–4a,

---

[1] (1952). The separate English translation is contained in Zimmerli and Jeremias, *The Servant of God* (London, 1957), and all page references are to this translation.

[2] See now the excellent discussion in Morna D. Hooker, *Jesus and the Servant, The influence of the Servant Concept of Deutero-Isaiah in the N.T.* (London, 1959), espec. 107–10, and C. F. D. Moule, *Studiorum Novi Testamenti Societas*, Bulletin III, 1952, 40ff, and *J.T.S.*, N.S., x (1959), 251f.

while Matthew himself has added to it from the LXX. The passage from Isaiah has been employed, it seems, to illustrate Jesus' desire to avoid publicity, and this it does very impressively. The use of the text can hardly be primitive, nor does it claim to be. It is simply a pious comment on a characteristic of Jesus' behaviour, made by someone who knew the Hebrew O.T. and desired to translate this portion for the benefit of a Greek-speaking congregation. He translated עֶבֶד by παῖς, as the LXX translators did, in order to avoid using a menial word in a passage where God is speaking so affectionately to his servant. Even if it was proved that Deutero-Isaiah was regarded as a purple passage by the Palestinian Church,[1] this one use of παῖς is not sufficient to show that it was regarded as the key word in this part of Isaiah. Nor does it prove that Deutero-Isaiah was the source for one of Jesus' titles, the significance of which was drawn from that context alone. If παῖς was regarded as the key word to these passages from Isaiah, we should expect to find in the N.T. many other citations of those parts of Deutero-Isaiah in which it stands, and we never do.[2] The words from heaven at Jesus' Baptism are held, by Jeremias and others, to embody a quotation from Isa. 42.1. Even if the thesis is accepted, and the evidence is not overwhelming, it proves not that the primitive Church had a Servant Christology, but rather that the servant element in the tradition, if it existed as a separate element at all, was so weak that it was very early transmuted into a Son Christology.

Certainly there is a theme of "humiliation and exaltation"[3] running through Acts, which passages from Deutero-Isaiah were used to illustrate. Since, however, the theme and the illustrations were used as often in the case of Paul as in the case of Jesus, it is unlikely that a specific Servant Christology lay behind it. While Isa. 53.7,8 was quoted by the Ethiopian Trea-

---

[1] The citation of Isa. 53.4 in Matt. 8.17 from the Hebrew shows that Isa. 53 was applied to Jesus, but so were many other O.T. passages.

[2] μορφὴν δούλου in Phil. 2.7 is the nearest.

[3] E. Schweizer, *Erniedrigung und Erhöhung bei Jesus und seinen Nachfolgern* (Zürich, 1955).

surer in Acts 8.32f and applied by Philip to Jesus, Isa. 49.6 was quoted by Paul in Acts 13.47 and applied to himself and Barnabas. Further, there may be an allusion to Isa. 48.6,7 in Acts 9.15, where God explained to Ananias that the mission for which he had chosen Paul would involve suffering, and would be a mission to the Gentiles and to kings, as well as to Israel. The working out of this theme in Acts is sufficient to explain the use of παῖς in Peter's speech in Acts 3. The association of the word with Isa. 52, where the persecuted παῖς is exalted, may have suggested it to Luke as a particularly appropriate Messianic designation to employ in reminding the Jews of what they had done to Jesus, but the reference to Isaiah is so weak that one can hardly base on this one verse a theory that there existed a distinct παῖς Christology which automatically invoked a whole set of images from the Isaianic servant passages. The use of the term in Acts 3 does nothing to weaken the evidence for the rest of Acts, that Luke understood παῖς to mean primarily "Son" or "Messiah", and that he was correctly reproducing the traditional meaning.

The most significant use of παῖς occurs in Acts 4.25,27,30, where Luke is directly in touch with traditional material. We know from Luke's Gospel how concerned he was with the duty of Christians to pray. For example, six times he added to the Marcan account the information that when Jesus withdrew he withdrew to pray, particularly when important decisions, like choosing the twelve Apostles, were in question.[1] We should expect, then, that he would have been particularly influenced by the liturgical language of his own Church.[2] This certainly is the case in the prayer of the Church in Acts 4, where David and Jesus are both called the Lord's παῖς. The same combination also occurs in the eucharistic prayer in the Didache (9.2), and Jesus is called God's παῖς in prayers from 1 Clement

---

[1] Luke 3.21, cf. Mark 1.9; Luke 5.16, cf. Mark 1.45; Luke 6.12, cf. Mark 3.13; Luke 9.18, cf. Mark 8.27; Luke 9.28f, cf. Mark 9.2f.

[2] A point worked out more fully by M. J. Wilcox, Ph.D. Thesis submitted to the University of Edinburgh (1955): *The Semitisms of Acts i–xv: A Critical and Linguistic Study.*

(59.2ff) the Martyrdom of Polycarp (14.1,3; 20.2, a doxology), and the Coptic version of the Didache (10.7). All these writings are independent of each other, and it is probably correct to conclude that they depended on a common liturgical tradition.

How ancient was this tradition? There is evidence that it had pre-Christian antecedents. Apart from translations of the O.T., David is only called God's servant in prayers, and it is possible that the Christian Church took over this tradition, which is found in both Palestinian and Dispersion sources.[1]

If we possess here a continuing tradition, present in pre-Christian as well as in Christian sources, we are in a much better position than usual to discover what was meant by παῖς. Beginning with Acts and the Didache, the most striking fact is that neither refers to Deutero-Isaiah. In Acts 4.25f the O.T. quotation comes from Psalm 2.1,2, and the one allusion to Isaiah, in the words ὅν ἔχρισας (Isa. 61.1), is not to a servant passage. In Did. 9.2 the allusion to the vine David spoke about probably goes back to Psalm 80.8ff (79.9 ff).[2] The connection made between David and Jesus is purely messianic, a point that is particularly clear in Acts, where Psalm 2 is used (see verse 7);[3] παῖς θεοῦ is simply another designation for the Messiah. This is in perfect accordance with the old prayers where David is called God's עֶבֶד or δοῦλος. In the two Greek examples, 1 Macc. 4.30 and 4 Ezra 3.23, it is recalled that David slew Goliath and founded Jerusalem, and "servant" is probably nothing more than a general title of honour. The three Palestinian examples, however, look forward to the coming of the Messiah, and are far more likely to have been the models for the Christian prayers. In each case "servant" occurs in parallelism or in close proximity to "Anointed One", and it is hard to avoid the conclusion that it means no more than "chosen by God". If the variant reading of the Babylonian recension of the XVIII Benedictions is accepted, it reads, "Let the righteous rejoice in the rebuilding of thy city and in the establishment of

---

1 Jeremias, op. cit., 48 n 184.
2 Ibid., 79 n 344.
3 Haenchen, op. cit., 169 n 4.

thy Temple, and in the flourishing of the horn of David thy servant, and in the clear shining light of the son of Jesse, thine anointed."[1] The old Musaf prayer interpolated into the XVIII Benedictions contains these words: זכרון משיח בן דוד עבדך "a remembrance of the anointed son of David thy servant", and the passover *haggada* וּבְמִקְחֲלוֹת before the fourth cup is, דוד בן־ ישי עבדך משיחך, "David, son of Jesse, thy servant, thine anointed."[2] All the evidence, both Jewish and Christian, suggests that in this context the common term "servant of God" meant "Messiah" and had no particular connection with the Book of Isaiah.

It is, then, possible that the Hebrew word עבד lay behind the liturgical use of παῖς, but the fact that the עבד stood in close relationship to "Messiah" in this tradition shows that the meaning of both עבד and παῖς must be taken from the context rather than from Deutero-Isaiah, to which there is no reference. In that case, παῖς is a particularly appropriate translation because it means "son" as well as "servant", and, as we shall argue later, "son of God" (in Luke at least) means simply "Messiah". The fact that παῖς was used to translate עבד in Deutero-Isaiah should probably be explained in the same way— the translator wished to avoid δοῦλος and thought that the intimate associations of παῖς were appropriate—and there is no evidence that the special context in Isaiah has had a particular influence on the N.T. use of παῖς. The same explanation might also illuminate the problem of the source of the words from heaven at Jesus' Baptism. If they were a free rendering of the Hebrew of Isa. 42.1, the translating of עבד by υἱός is no longer surprising: עבד in this context was rightly taken to be a messianic designation, and correctly translated "son". The translator had no conception of a separate "Servant Christology".

Perhaps, however, the old prayer tradition that Jesus, like David, was called God's παῖς carried with it allusions to his

---

[1] Tr. A. Cohen, *The Babylonian Talmud: Tractate Bᵉrākōt* (Cambridge, 1921), 192.

[2] All three prayers are reproduced in Jeremias, op. cit., 48 n 184.

10

death, simply because Jesus had interpreted his death in terms of the servant passages in Deutero-Isaiah. Jeremias has collected about a dozen examples from the Gospels which he believes show that Jesus had thought about his death in the light of Isa. 53, but in most of these it is very difficult to see any allusion to Isaiah; the supposed allusions are either common expressions elsewhere, or are sufficiently explained by the context without reference to Isaiah.[1] There is only one direct quotation, Luke 22.37, which must be attributed to the theological reflection of the Church on what had happened. Even at the level of later theological reflection, as G. Bornkamm has remarked, the passion Psalms are much more prominent than Isaiah ever became.[2] The conclusion seems to be that Jesus never explicitly referred to Deutero-Isaiah, and that it only became popular as a proof-text rather later in the history of the Church. Paul has one allusion to Isa. 53 (Rom. 4.25); it is quoted in 1 Pet. 2.22–5 and Heb. 9.28, in 1 Clem. 16.2–14 and Barn. 5.2, and then in glorious profusion in Justin Martyr (29 times).[3] On this count, too, Luke-Acts takes its place with the later Christian writings.

The discussion of the meaning of παῖς has shown that there are no grounds for believing that the primitive Church had a separate Servant Christology. In the N.T. contexts the word is simply another title of honour with messianic implications. It originally had no special reference to Deutero-Isaiah; if Isaiah was quoted at Jesus' baptism, the reference here, as in the David prayer-tradition, was simply to the close relationship existing between God and his Messiah; Matthew's traditional material has employed a servant passage from Isaiah only to illustrate Jesus' avoidance of publicity; Luke perhaps had Isa. 52.13 (LXX) in mind when he used the phrase ἐδόξασεν τὸν παῖδα αὐτοῦ in Acts 3.13, but there is no evidence that this is either

---

[1] Jeremias, op. cit., 98–104. The passages covered by the explanations above are: Mark 2.20 par.; Mark 9.12; Luke 11.22; Mark 10.45 par; Mark 14.8; Mark 14.24 par; John 10.11,15,17f (cf. P. Oxy., I recto 19f).

[2] Op. cit., 144,205; E. Schweizer, op. cit., 81ff.

[3] According to the *Index locorum* in Goodspeed's edition (Göttingen, 1914).

primitive or significant for the basic meaning of the word. Those O.T. passages which we now distinguish as "servant" passages became available for the illustration of the theme of Jesus' humiliation and glorification after παῖς had been established as a Christological title; they did not form the starting point for a so-called Servant Christology.

Again the evidence shows that Luke stood rather late in the stream of theological development, though he has incorporated an ancient tradition. Perhaps because he was aware of the ancient lineage of the Christological term παῖς, he confined its use to the early chapters of Acts. In this his usage accords with that of the Apostolic Fathers, where it was usually confined to prayers. There is evidence from the Epistle of Barnabas that it was then regarded as an archaic title with O.T. overtones, in that παῖς was inserted into two citations from the O.T. to provide an explicit reference to Christ (Bar. 6.1, Isa. 50.8,9; Bar. 9.2, Ex. 15.26). This is also evidence that the title was in use rather late in the history of the early Church.[1]

The remaining titles may be treated more briefly. Luke, like Mark, understood ὁ υἱὸς τοῦ θεοῦ to mean simply "Messiah".[2] This is most clearly seen in Luke 4.41, a composite passage in which the author is dependent on both Mark 1.34 and 3.10f.: "And demons also came out of a number of them, crying out, 'You are the Son of God!' But he rebuked them and would not let them speak, because they knew that he was the Messiah." It can also be shown from Luke 22.70; Acts 9.20 (cf. 22); and 13.33 (a citation from Ps. 2.7).

There is no need to discuss what was originally meant by the title ὁ υἱὸς τοῦ ἀνθρώπου. The evidence from the Gospel,

---

[1] The frequent use of the adjectives ἀγαπητός and ἠγαπημένος with παῖς in the Apostolic Fathers (1 Clem. 59.2,3; Diog. 8.11; Mar.Polyc. 14.1,3), which slides into μονογενής in Mar. Polyc. 20.2 (cf. Diog. 8.9; μόνῳ τῷ παιδί), is due to the influence of the words from heaven at Jesus' Baptism and Transfiguration. It is further evidence to show that παῖς was understood primarily to mean "son", even if these adjectives may originally have come from Isa. 42.1; 44.2 (and 41.8?).

[2] Cadbury, *Beginnings*, v.363.

especially from the account of Jesus' trial, suggests that Luke regarded it as the hidden messianic title, the only one which in Jesus' reticence about his messiahship he would allow to pass his lips. After the resurrection there was no longer any need for the cryptic title "Son of Man": It was used only by the Seer (Rev. 1.13; 14.14) and the two martyrs, Stephen and James the Just.[1] Without arguing that the two martyr traditions are dependent on one another in any way, this coincidence does at least show that there was a tradition abroad that the early martyrs in Jerusalem confessed that Jesus was the Son of Man before they died. Perhaps this is the one title in Acts for which there is definite evidence that it was actually used at the time and place assigned to it in the narrative. All the other titles were current in Luke's own generation, and he has given them their positions in the speeches according to his idea of the historical probability that they would have been used under those circumstances, and according to his own theological point of view.

The title ὁ Ναζωραῖος seems to imply no more than that Jesus came from Nazareth.[2] This is clear from comparing Peter's speech to a Roman in Acts 10.38, where he says Ἰησοῦν τὸν ἀπὸ Ναζαρέθ, with his speech to Jews in 2.22, where he says Ἰησοῦν τόν Ναζωραῖον. There remains a difficulty in seeing why it should have been used by enemies of Christianity to give a subversive flavour to their charges (6.14; 24.5 in the plural, "the sect of the Nazarenes").

The rather nebulous titles ὁ ἅγιος, ὁ ὅσιος, and ὁ δίκαιος are probably not primitive, and provide interesting evidence of the way in which Christological titles developed in Luke's period.

The first two probably originated as adjectives. In Mark

---

[1] Hippolytus in Eus., *H.E.*, ii.23.13; ?Gospel according to the Hebrews in Jerome, *De vir. ill.*, 2. H. J. Schoeps, *Theologie und Geschichte des Judenchristentums* (Tübingen, 1949), Excursus v, 438–44, argues that Luke had taken over the speech and martyrdom of James and given it to Stephen in order to minimize its anti-cultish effect. As we have argued in Chapter Three, there is no minimizing involved.

[2] F. F. Bruce, op. cit. (London, 1951), 90.

1.24; Luke 4.34 ὁ ἅγιος τοῦ θεοῦ is an adjectival use, and a comparison with Luke 4.41 shows that it is another way of describing the Messiah. It was elevated to a title in Acts 3.14. The title ὁ ὅσιος (Acts 2.27; 13.35), if it can be called a title, came from the LXX, Psalm 16(15).10, where it was used adjectivally. The general tendency for this sort of adjective to be turned into a title can be illustrated from other Christian writings from the same period as Acts. The term παῖς, which has already been discussed, never became an independent title, "the servant", and was always qualified by a possessive pronoun, "my servant" or "his servant", until the time of the Epistle to Diognetus (8.9,11; 9.1). In the Apocalypse the adjective ὅσιος was transformed into a title for God in the process of quoting from Psalm 145(144).17 (Rev. 16.5 according to the best manuscripts). The same effect may perhaps also be discerned in Rev. 3.7, where the Son of God is called ὁ ἅγιος, ὁ ἀληθινός. Finally, Luke himself showed this tendency when he alone of the early writers who used ἀρχηγός did so without a qualifying genitive; the result was to turn a description into a title.[1]

The adjective δίκαιος probably became a title in much the same way. It is a title in Acts 22.14, if not in 3.14 and 7.52, but otherwise there is no other example of its use in this way in either the N.T. or the Apostolic Fathers.[2] "The righteous man" is referred to in the O.T. and in the Wisdom of Solomon, but this is not sufficient to explain the title, nor is the fact that the Messiah is called "righteous", although this brings the possibility closer. The Qumrân writings, besides mentioning the Teacher of Righteousness, or rather the Righteous Teacher (מורה הצדק), also speak of the righteous (or legitimate) Messiah (משיח הצדק).[3] The Rabbis also applied such phrases as Zech.

---

[1] Acts 5.31; cf. Acts 3.15; Heb. 2.10; 12.2; 1 Clem. 14.1; 51.1; 2 Clem. 20.5; Eus., *H.E.*, v.2.3; which are discussed below.

[2] Jas. 5.6 is not a title.

[3] F. M. Cross, *The Ancient Library of Qumrân and Modern Biblical Studies* (London, 1958), 83 and n 3; citing 4Q Patriarchal Blessings, line 3. Perhaps 1 John 2.1 repeats this sort of phrase.

9.9, "he is just and having salvation" to the Messiah.[1] It seems that the only pre-Christian writing actually to employ the title "The Righteous One" for the Messiah is the (Ethiopian) Book of Enoch (38.2; 53.6). Enoch is probably quoted by the Epistle of Barnabas (En. 89.55,66f in Barn. 16.5), so that it is possible that this is the source of the title in Luke. It seems more likely, however, that both Enoch and Acts have arrived at the title by the same process of deducing a title from an adjectival description. Perhaps further influences at work are the tendency to make a singular title for Jesus out of a plural description of his followers,[2] and Luke's predilection for a word which carries the implication of innocence.[3]

The evidence that these three titles were current in the primitive Church is lacking, and there is positive evidence for ἅγιος and δίκαιος that they were common titles at a later period in the Church's life. In 1 Clem. 23.5 ὁ ἅγιος is inserted into a quotation from Mal. 3.1 to supply an explicit reference to Christ, showing that the term was in use at that time but was felt to have the sort of archaic character which would fit it for this purpose. It has already been noted that ὁ δίκαιος is never used as a title for Jesus in either the N.T. or the Apostolic Fathers apart from Acts. In Justin's Dialogue with Trypho, however, we find not only the same title but the same context. The word is used as a title four times (16.4; 17.1; 119.3; 136.2), each time as part of the charge against the Jews. "For you have killed the Righteous One and the prophets before him. And now you reject those who hope in him and in Him who sent him, God the sovereign and creator of all. As far as you can, you insult and curse in your synagogues those who believe in the Messiah. You have no power to lay hands on us because of the present rulers, but what you are able to do you do" (16.4).

---

[1] Schrenk, art. δίκαιος in Kittel, *Th.Wb.z.N.T.*, ii.188; for the rabbinic comment on Zech. 9.9 see Pesikt. R. 34 (159b).

[2] Cf. ὁ ἐκλεκτός, Luke 22.35; John 1.34 v.l.; of David, 1 Clem. 52.2. But this is also a messianic title in Enoch (40.5; 45.3f; 49.2,4; 51.3,5; 53.6, etc.).

[3] *Beginnings*, v.364 and n 3; Schrenk art. cit., 190f; Kilpatrick, *J.T.S.*, xliii (1942), 34–6.

The sentence from Isa. 3.10 (LXX), "Let us bind the righteous man, for he is distasteful to us" is quoted once in this context (136.2); it appears three times elsewhere in the Dialogue; and it was quoted in Bar. 6.7; which supports the suggestion that the O.T. passages where "the righteous man" is mentioned have played a part in elevating the adjective to a messianic title (cf. Dial. 16.4 quoting Isa. 57.1). In Chapter One we have argued that Justin Martyr did not know Luke-Acts, while sharing many of Luke's most important theological presuppositions. The use of the title ὁ δίκαιος in the same sort of context may now be added to the list of less important points of agreement between the two.

The final pair of titles to be considered is ἀρχηγός and σωτήρ. It is very likely that these two words go together in early Christian theological traditions, and that they have been imported into Christianity ultimately, if not directly, from Hellenistic religious sources.[1] They occur together in one form or another in Acts 5.31, Heb. 2.10, and 2 Clem. 20.5. The last two instances have to do with the achievement of life out of death, a thought which appears as the context of ἀρχηγός in Acts 3.15 and the Martyrdom of Lyons (Eusebius, *H.E.*, v.2.3), and as the context of σωτήρ in 2 Tim. 1.10 and Diogn. 9.6. There seems to be a good case for claiming that all these passages reflect a common theological tradition of the saving work of Christ. None of them, except perhaps the Martyrdom of Lyons,[2] seems to be directly dependent on any of the others. They are all second century writings.

Acts 3.15. "You killed the *originator* (or Prince) of life."

Acts 5.31. "This Jesus God exalted to his right hand as *Prince* and *Saviour*, to give Israel repentance and forgiveness of sins."

[1] For ἀρχηγός both E. Schweizer, op. cit., 30 n 108, and H. Conzelmann, *Die Mitte der Zeit* (Tübingen, 1954), 179 n 1 cite W. G. Kümmel, *Kirchenbegriff und Geschichtsbewusstsein in der Urgemeinde und bei Jesus* (1943), 12 and 17, which I have been unable to see. For σωτήρ see H. Conzelmann in Dibelius, *Die Pastoralbriefe, Hdb.z.N.T.* (3rd ed., Tübingen, 1955), 74-7.

[2] Cadbury thinks Eus., *H.E.*, v.2.5, may be a quotation from Acts; *The Book of Acts in History* (London, 1955), 158 and n 45.

2 Tim. 1.10. "Grace . . . has now been revealed through the appearing of our *Saviour* Jesus Christ, who disarmed death and through the gospel brought to light life and incorruption."

Heb. 2.10. "It is proper that in leading many sons to glory he for whom and by whom all things exist should make the *originator* of their *salvation* perfect through sufferings."

2 Clem. 20.5. "To the only unseen God, the Father of truth, who sent us the *Saviour* and *originator* of immortality, through whom he also revealed to us the truth and the heavenly life, to him be glory for ever and ever. Amen."

Diogn. 9.6. "Therefore when he had demonstrated the inability of our nature before then to achieve life, he now has revealed the *Saviour* who is able to save, even where it was impossible . . ."

Eus., *H.E.*, v.2.3. "For they gladly conceded the title of 'Martyr' to Christ, the faithful and true martyr, the firstborn of the dead and *originator* of the life of God."

The idea has naturally been thoroughly christianized, but probably we have to do with a complex of themes taken over from oriental and Hellenistic saviour cults and the mystery religions, perhaps through the medium of Hellenistic Judaism.[1] The ideas had taken root, however, only because the soil was prepared. Σωτήρ is an O.T. term for God (see Luke 1.47) and may have been a messianic designation (Enoch 48.7; XVIII Benedictions, etc.),[2] and as "Jesus" in Hebrew means "Yahweh is salvation" the title Saviour would immediately seem relevant to him (Acts 13.23; cf. Matt. 1.21). Nothing could be further from the mystery religions, with their emphasis on the enlightenment and enlivening of the initiates, than Luke's historical and prosaic theology,[3] but in this case his vocabulary unwittingly betrays the foreign influence.

[1] Cf. Philo, *Leg. All.*, iii.27; *Conf. Ling.* 93, quoted for σωτήρ by Conzelmann, op. cit., 76.

[2] Conzelmann, ibid., 75.

[3] Conzelmann, *Die Mitte der Zeit*, 178f and 202 (Eng. tr., 205f and 230) argues that Luke means nothing more by ἀρχηγὸς τῆς ζωῆς than πρῶτος ἐξ ἀναστάσεως (Acts 26.23).

The conjunction of unusual Christological terms around chapters 3, 4, and 5 of Acts is quite remarkable; there we find παῖς, ἀρχηγός, and ἅγιος; ὁ Ναζωραῖος appears twice (five times elsewhere), δίκαιος once (twice elsewhere) and σωτήρ once (once elsewhere). This has led commentators to conclude that they had suddenly struck a rich vein of early Christology, a pocket of ideas which was soon abandoned because of restrictions imposed by orthodoxy. Unfortunately that is too simple an explanation. All these terms, and the others we have examined, have a diverse history, but all, with the possible exception of κύριος and the pair we have just discussed, were by Luke's time different ways of calling Jesus "Messiah". The diversity of their history shows that they did not come to Luke straight from an old source which recorded the primitive speeches. Some of the terms, like χριστός, κύριος, παῖς, υἱὸς τοῦ θεοῦ, and υἱὸς τοῦ ἀνθρώπου, were very old; they had come down to Luke in various ways, and had sometimes undergone shifts of meaning. Others, like δίκαιος, ἅγιος, and ὅσιος, were relatively late. Finally, in ἀρχηγός and σωτήρ we have found terms with a long pagan history which is now scarcely discernible in the sober pages of Acts.

Chapters 3, 4, and 5 provide an exuberance of uncommon titles because Luke is striving to give an archaic and scriptural ring to that part of Acts where a final appeal is made to the Jews in Jerusalem to accept their Messiah. His purpose in using these terms is to demonstrate that Christianity had inherited the finest aspirations of Israel, but without knowing it he shows how far the Church had developed away from Judaism, and how different the issues between them had become. Both Christianity and Judaism had changed.

# CHAPTER SIX

# THE DEBT TO HELLENISTIC JUDAISM

WE HAVE learnt a great deal about Luke from comparing his views with those of the Christian theologians who, we have reason to believe, were his contemporaries. Our task will not be complete, however, until we know the wider background of his thought. We need to look beyond Christianity to Judaism which, as Luke's own theological interests have already suggested, still provided the ethos for Christian thinking.

There is a strong case for saying that the Judaism to which Luke was indebted was not Palestinian Judaism but the Judaism of the Dispersion. It rests on his use of the Septuagint. As W. K. L. Clarke has shown in his article on "The Use of the LXX in Acts",[1] a high proportion of the words peculiar to Luke-Acts (51 out of 58) and a high proportion of the words characteristic of Luke-Acts (68 out of 69) occur in the LXX. This alone might only prove that Luke was very familiar with his Greek Bible, but the number of special affinities Clarke has shown to exist between Luke-Acts and the apocryphal books of the O.T. indicates that the literature peculiar to Greek-speaking Judaism has exerted a particular influence on his thought. Not only is the LXX his authoritative text of the O.T.—James's argument in Acts 15.17 would not hold if the Hebrew scriptures were employed[2]—but those parts of it which did not exist in Hebrew have coloured the language of his narrative.[3]

The Judaism of the Dispersion had for at least three centuries

---

[1] *Beginnings*, ii.66–105.

[2] Despite Torrey, *Composition and Date of Acts* (Cambridge, Mass., 1916), 38f; see E. Haenchen, "Tradition und Komposition in der Apg.", *Z.Th.K.*, 52 (1955), 208.

[3] Ibid., 73–80.

been confronted with the sort of missionary problem which the Church faced in the first century of its life. It had produced a large body of missionary literature written in Greek which employed a developed apologetic to convince its Gentile readers of the truth of the Jewish faith.[1] We know that some of these writings were prized by Christians—the only remnants of Demetrius, Philo the Elder, Eupolemus, Artapanos, Ezekiel the Tragedian, and Aristobulos are to be found in Eusebius or Clement of Alexandria[2]—and one of their favourite arguments, that the Greeks learnt their philosophy from Moses, soon became a stock piece of Christian apologetic, but it is still a matter of debate how early this Hellenistic Jewish thought made its mark on Christian theology. In this chapter we shall ask whether a number of features of Acts cannot best be explained by assuming that the Church to which Luke belonged had learnt much of both its missionary strategy and its missionary theology from the Synagogues of the Dispersion.

Although we shall bring forward a number of detailed comparisons between Hellenistic Jewish missionary literature and Acts, it is important to note that the influence of this literature is not confined to the details but affects the whole. Luke is not only influenced in the way he describes the missionary activity of his heroes by the practice of the Synagogues in proselytizing among their Gentile neighbours, but his work is itself an argument for the faith, which he hoped would be read by non-Christians as well as by Christians. It should be compared as a whole with the apologetic writings of Hellenistic Judaism.

We should not expect Luke's purpose of converting men to Christianity to be immediately obvious. He would not be an

---

[1] Peter Dalbert, *Die Theologie der hellenistisch-jüdischen Missions-literatur unter Ausschluss von Philo und Josephus* (Hamburg, 1954). To his list should be added *The Life and Confession, or Prayer of Asenath*, text edited by P. Batiffol, *Studia Patristica* (Fascicule 1,2, Paris, 1889–90); see Kaufmann Kohler, *The Jewish Encyclopedia*, ii (N.Y., 1902), 172–6; G. D. Kilpatrick, *E.T.*, 64 (1952–53), 4–8, accepted by J. Jeremias, Bultmann Festschrift (*Z.N.W.* Beiheft 21, Berlin 1954), 255, 260.

[2] Eusebius copied his extracts (except for Aristobulos) from Alexander Polyhistor's *Concerning the Jews*; Clement of Alexandria may have used the same source.

effective apologist if it was. The studied objectivity of the introduction to the whole work, and the comparisons it invites with the dedications to secular histories guarantee the seriousness of his missionary purpose.[1] In this he is following the Hellenistic Jewish tradition. Philo begins his *Life of Moses*, a work with a similar purpose, almost casually: "I hope to bring the story of this greatest and most perfect of men to the knowledge of such as deserve not to remain in ignorance of it; for, while the fame of the laws which he left behind him has travelled throughout the civilized world and reached the ends of the earth, the man himself as he really was is known to few."[2] Josephus, in the introduction to his *Jewish Antiquities* simply asks his Greek readers to approach his work with an open mind: "to fix their thoughts on God, and to test whether our lawgiver has had a worthy conception of his nature".[3]

The mention of Josephus, a Palestinian Jew who needed help with his Greek,[4] might seem to weaken the case that Hellenistic Judaism is the main influence on Luke's method, but it should be observed that Josephus himself appeals to the apologetic writings of his Greek-speaking Dispersion compatriots in justifying his undertaking. After mentioning the traditional story about the request of Ptolemy II for the co-operation of the High Priest Eleazar in producing the Septuagint, he writes, "Accordingly, I thought that it became me also to imitate the high priest's magnanimity and to assume there are still to-day many lovers of learning like the king."[5] Josephus has also taken his model from the apologetic experience of Hellenistic Judaism.[6]

---

[1] H. J. Cadbury is right to insist that the avowed purpose of Luke 1.1–4 is "to correct misinformation about Christianity rather than, as is so often supposed, to confirm the historical basis of Theophilus's religious faith"; *The Making of Luke-Acts* (N.Y. 1927), 315; cf. *Beginnings*, ii.489–510.

[2] *De vita Mosis*, 1 (tr. F. H. Colson, Loeb Library, London and Cambridge, Mass., 1935), 277.

[3] Proem 3 (tr. H. St. J. Thackeray, Loeb Library, 1930), 9.

[4] Ap. i.50; see H. St. J. Thackeray, *Josephus, the Man and the Historian* (N.Y., 1929), 5th Lecture.

[5] Tr. Thackeray, op cit., 7.

[6] Josephus has a Palestinian forerunner in Eupolemos, who lived in the middle of the second century B.C.: Eus. *Praep.Ev.*, ix.26,30–34,39 (cf. Clem.

Perhaps it is Luke's familiarity—or the familiarity of the makers of the Christian tradition to which he belonged—with the apologetic literature of Hellenistic Judaism that led him to adopt the form of a history for his work. It is, after all, not immediately obvious that a history of the Church would be the best way to commend Christianity to unbelievers. A philosophical argument or a discourse about the moral teaching of Jesus might have been more immediately attractive to a cultured audience. In choosing to write the history of the foundation period of the Church Luke has chosen the basic method which the Greek-speaking Jewish apologists had chosen before him. Demetrius, Artapanos, and Eupolemos simply recounted the history of the Patriarchs, with more or less elaboration; the writer of the Wisdom of Solomon meditated on the significance of the Exodus;[1] Aristobulus and Philo, though eager to put the discussion on a philosophical plane, started from the history and character of Moses and the other leaders of their people; Ezekiel the Tragedian wrote *The Exodus*, a historical drama; and *The Prayer of Asenath* was the story of an ideal conversion to Judaism based on the historical fact that Joseph married the daughter of an Egyptian priest. The lesson in all these works was that God had manifestly worked in the history of Israel. It has required the essays of Dibelius to drive home the simple fact that Acts is designed to show the same thing for the early history of the Church.[2] However much the theological understanding of the history of God's people belongs to the essence of Jewish and Christian faith, it must still be recognized that the decision to attempt to win converts by expounding this special history to unbelievers was a new step, and a step taken in the environment where the Septuagint was made.

The thesis that Luke has been affected by that apologetic

---

Alex., *Str.*, i.23.153; 21.130); W. N. Stearns, *Fragments from Graeco-Jewish Writers* (Chicago, 1908), 29–41; Dalbert, op. cit.,35–42. One of his arguments is that Moses was the πρῶτος σοφός who gave the alphabet to the Greeks through the Phoenicians (Eus., *Praep. Ev.*, ix.26).

[1] At least, the writer of Sap. Sal. 11–19; see Dalbert, op. cit., 71 f.

[2] Cadbury, *The Making of Luke-Acts* (N.Y. 1927), 303–6, made the same point.

tradition can only be sustained if it can be shown in the details that Acts is indebted to the methods employed by Jewish missionary writers who wrote in Greek. There are four points at which this is possible, although one cannot always say that Hellenistic Jewish missionary literature provides the only parallel. The four points are: the way Acts commends the heroes of the faith; the appeal to the State; the approach to the philosophers; and the theology of conversion.

On two occasions in Acts Paul is taken to be a god by a heathen people, the first time at Lystra when he is called Hermes and Barnabas Zeus (14.11f), and the second time on Malta when he suffers no ill-effects from snake-bite (28.6).

The incident at Lystra can scarcely be historical. Assuming the Lystrans to have been among the recipients of the Epistle to the Galatians, appeal has been made to Gal. 4.14 for the basis of this narrative: ὡς ἄγγελον θεοῦ ἐδέξασθέ με. In fact the contrast between the two passages could scarely be more telling. In his Epistle Paul praises the original discernment of the Galatians in accepting him as God's messenger, ὡς Χριστὸν Ἰησοῦν, despite his weakness of the flesh; in Acts a display of wonder-working power drives the poor credulous Lystrans to do sacrifice to the two apostles. The chief difficulty which lies in the way of accepting this story as historical is the unlikeli-hood that either the Lystrans or the priest of Zeus would honour Barnabas and Paul as gods simply because they had performed a cure. They would have honoured successful Jewish exorcists, but not honoured them as gods.[1] If the story is unlikely to have occurred, we must try to understand how Luke came to con-struct it.

This is the first time in Acts that any Christian missionaries have come into contact with a Gentile audience which has not been prepared for the gospel in the Synagogue, and it is inter-esting to see that the teaching given to them by Paul makes no mention of Christ; this is a common apologetic opportunity which would be familiar to Hellenistic Jews, and Barnabas

---

[1] A Loisy, *Les Actes des Apôtres* (Paris, 1920), 552; Haenchen, op. cit., 380.

and Paul meet it in a typical way. The point of the speech is that there is one God, the Creator, far above all the so-called gods who are like men. Luke has given magnificent dramatic support to this argument by letting the Lycaonians demonstrate the absurdity of their worship when they try to sacrifice to Barnabas and Paul. He is dramatizing the ridicule with which Jews since Second Isaiah had regarded the religions which honoured idols and gods that were plainly unworthy of honour when compared with the "living God who made heaven and earth and the sea and all that is in them".

Part of the occasion for constructing this scene was offered by the legend that Zeus and Hermes had appeared to Baucis and Philemon in this district.[1] Luke puts Paul into the rôle of Hermes, traditionally the messenger of the gods. It is unlikely at this early stage in the work of Paul that he would do all the talking while Barnabas kept silent, but the title "leader in speaking" is a good description of Paul's status in Acts as a whole, besides having another sense which the readers of Acts would quickly see: leading exponent of the Word of God.[2] Nor is Luke deterred from applying this title to Paul here by the fact that, although Hermes carried messages for Zeus, he would not do so while Zeus was present.[3] It seems that he has begun to construct a story with the intention of showing both that Paul's position as a preacher was recognized by pagans, and that the recognition of his position was spoiled by their propensity to worship the creature in place of the Creator. The local legend about Zeus and Hermes was probably the means by which the story was elaborated, but a basic element is still unexplained. Why should Luke ever imagine that pagans would honour the heroes of the faith as gods?

[1] Ovid, *Metamorphoses*, viii.611–724. The Lystran inscriptions discovered by Prof. W. M. Calder which link Zeus and Hermes show that Ovid's legend had a basis in the religious practice of the area, but do not prove that the story in Acts is historical; cf. F. F. Bruce, *The Acts of the Apostles* (London, 1951), 281f.

[2] Hermes is called θεὸς ὁ τῶν λόγων ἡγεμών in Jamblichus, *De mysteriis Aegypt.*, 1; for further parallels see Bauer-Arndt-Gingrich, 310, 344.

[3] Loisy, op. cit., 551; Haenchen, op. cit., 379.

The legendary account of Moses in the Hellenistic Jewish missionary story by Artapanos called *Concerning the Jews* offers an analogy and an explanation.[1] Artapanos makes a great deal of the achievement of Moses in ruling over the Egyptians; he says that he taught Orpheus, invented ships and machines for use in peace and war, and invented philosophy.[2] Even more surprising is his reorganization of the religious life of Egypt, in which he provided the priests with their sacred writings so that the kingdom would be safe and law-abiding. "For these reasons, then, Moses was beloved by the multitudes, and being deemed by the priests worthy to be honoured like a god, was named Hermes, because of his interpretation of the Hieroglyphics (διὰ τὴν τῶν ἱερῶν γραμμάτων ἑρμηνείαν)."[3]

Artapanos's book is a good example of the apologetic desire to show that the great leaders in the history of the Jews were highly honoured, even deified, by the non-Jews they met. Luke's two accounts of the way pagans honoured Paul as a god, particularly the second occasion on Malta, serve the same purpose, and both the motive and the device may well have been inherited from the Hellenistic Jewish tradition of apologetics. Certainly, if he knew the old legend that the Egyptians called Moses Hermes, he would then have to hand the suggestion necessary for constructing the scene which he sets in Lystra.

Artapanos provides another possible parallel to Acts in his account of Moses' miraculous release from prison.

"And when the king of Egypt heard of the arrival of Moses, he called him before him, and asked what he had come for: and he said, Because the Lord of the world (τῆς οἰκουμένης δεσπότην) commanded him to deliver the Jews.

And when the king heard this, he shut him up in prison. But when it was night, all the doors of the prison-house opened of their own accord (τάς τε θύρας πάσας αὐτομάτως ἀνοιχθῆναι τοῦ δεσμωτηρίου), and of the guards some died, and some were sunk in sleep, and their weapons broken in pieces."[4]

---

[1] Eus., *Praep. Ev.*, ix.18,23,27; cf. Clem. Alex., *Strom.*, i.23.154; Stearns, op. cit., 42–56; see Dalbert, op. cit., 42–52.   [2] Eus., ix.27.
[3] Ibid., tr. Gifford (Oxford, 1903), iii. 463.   [4] Ibid., tr. Gifford, 465.

Acts contains three miraculous releases from prison (5.18ff, the Apostles; 12.5–10, Peter; 16.22–8, Paul and Silas) and the account in Artapanos is similar to the first two.[1] Clarke has pointed out the similarity between the language of the third and the *Testament of Joseph*, though this of course contains no miraculous release.[2] We may conclude that, at least in the telling of the stories, Luke is in debt to Hellenistic Jewish literature.

Acts is designed to show that Christianity is a law-abiding religion and that it should be recognized as such by the Roman state.[3] The Hellenistic synagogues had everywhere been officially recognized, but they could never be sure that their political privileges would not at any moment be disregarded or withdrawn. Their apologetic writings reflect this uncertainty and can profitably be compared with Acts.

Philo and Josephus both had direct dealings with the Romans and both wrote books which, in part at least, were intended to regain and confirm Roman toleration for the Jewish people. Philo's immediate concern was to avert the pogrom which was about to be launched on the Jewish settlement in Alexandria and which the prefect Flaccus was permitting and even encouraging. Larger issues immediately became involved, and Philo found himself writing on behalf of all Jewry to defend them from the necessity of worshipping the Emperor.[4] Josephus is writing under more difficult conditions, after the destruction of Jerusalem in A.D. 70, and his first attempt to regain the confidence of the Romans in his people had to be a warning to all subject peoples not to follow the example of the Jews and revolt against the Empire.[5] His *Antiquities*, on the other hand, was

---

[1] E. Preuschen, *Die Apg.*, *Hdb.z.N.T.* (Tübingen, 1912), 77: "This might have been the model here" (12.10).

[2] *Beginnings*, ii.77f.

[3] One of the firmly established points in the history of the criticism of Acts, it was early agreed upon by both sides of the Tübingen controversy: Schneckenburger and Zeller.

[4] *In Flaccum* and *De legatione ad Caium*; see E. R. Goodenough, *The Politics of Philo Judaeus, Practice and Theory* (New Haven, 1938).

[5] H. St J. Thackeray, op. cit., 2nd lecture, esp. 27–30.

"designed to magnify the Jewish race in the eyes of the Graeco-Roman world by a record of their ancient and glorious history".[1] In it he took care to mention the Roman records relating to the privileges which had been bestowed on the Jews.

Theology is not far from the surface in the apologies. Philo, particularly in *Against Flaccus*, makes it clear that any official who allows the Jews to be persecuted does so at his own risk. God defends his own, as Josephus reminds his readers in the Preface to the *Antiquities*. In the *Wisdom of Solomon* the "rulers of the earth" who are addressed in 1.1ff and 6.1ff might well ponder the fate of the Egyptians who persecuted the Jews.

> For they deserved to be deprived of light and kept
>     in darkness,
> They who kept imprisoned thy children
> Through whom the incorruptible light of the Law was
>     to be given to the world.  (18.4)[2]

Acts itself gives a purely Jewish account of the fate suffered by Herod Agrippa I. He is struck down because men had begun to deify him and, it may be inferred, because he persecuted the Church (Acts 12. esp. 20–3). No Roman official suffers because he harms the Church, but no Roman official persecutes the Church except from weakness or cupidity. Luke is not in the position of his Hellenistic Jewish fore-runners, who could appeal to a long history of legal recognition; he is asking for something the Church has never had, and is in no position to threaten the wrath of God if it is not granted.

The Apologists were not only defending their people and trying to show that God had defended them and would defend them. They carried their missionary zeal into the realm of politics, and dared to preach to their heathen overlords that only in the service of the true and living God could they learn how to rule properly. From the crude glorification of Joseph and Moses as model rulers who reorganized the whole system of Egyptian government in Artapanos to Philo's philosophical

---

[1] Ibid., 51.
[2] Dalbert, op. cit., 72f.

argument that Moses was the ideal king, [1] the Jewish apologists again and again put forward their law as the proper law for the ordering of human society.

The *Wisdom of Solomon*, though cast in markedly Greek terms, makes a strong appeal to rulers to recognize that their power stemmed from the one true God. It begins "Love righteousness, you judges of the earth", and in chapter six we read:

> Hear then, O kings, and consider,
> Learn, you judges of the earth.
> Listen, you who rule many peoples
> And have boasted of hosts of nations.
> Because your dominion was bestowed by the Lord,
> And your sovereignty by the Most High,
> He will put your works under review and
>    find out your plans,
> For you, who are servants of his Kingdom,
>    have not judged rightly,
> Have not kept the Law,
> And have not followed the will of God. . . .
> My words are for you, O rulers,
> So that you may learn wisdom and not
>    err.   (6.1–4,9)

The *Letter of Aristeas* is another interesting example of the same sort of claim. It relates how the ruler of Egypt desired to have a copy of the Hebrew scriptures in his library and sent to Jerusalem to the high priest to provide him with a translation. The supposed author of the book, who is writing this account for his friend Philocrates, is sent to Jerusalem with the king's request. He had previously prevailed on Pharaoh to release the Jews who were kept as slaves in Egypt, as a sign of devotion to the God whose scriptures he wanted to have translated. "Since the law which we want not only to transcribe but to

---

[1] "In God's foreknowledge he became king and lawgiver and high priest and prophet, and in each he was supreme (τὰ πρωτεῖα)"; *de vita Mosis*, ii.3.

translate belongs to all the Jews, how can we justify our mission while so many of them are kept in slavery in your kingdom? But in the perfection and bounty of your being, release those who are oppressed and suffer great hardship, for the God who holds you responsible for this kingdom is the God who gave them the Law (κατευθύνοντός σου τὴν βασιλείαν τοῦ τεθεικότος αὐτοῖς θεοῦ τὸν νόμον), as I have taken trouble to confirm. For they worship God the Guardian and Creator of all, whom all men, including ourselves, O king, call by different names, such as Zeus or Dis" . . . (15,16). This is very close to syncretism, but the boldness of writing Jewish propaganda under the name of a cultured Egyptian court official justifies the risk. The learned discourse of the seventy translators at the king's banquets, which occupies the bulk of the rest of the work, shows quite clearly that the Jews are the only exponents of the wisdom of the true God. At the end of one day's after-dinner discussions Aristeas writes: "The king saluted them in a loud voice and congratulated them, all present joining in the applause, especially the philosophers. For they greatly excelled the philosophers both in conduct and in argument because they made God their starting point (τὴν καταρχήν)" (235). The purpose is to show that in questions of conduct, especially the conduct of rulers and men of position, the Law of the God of the Jews is the best guide.

We may seem to have wandered away from the Book of Acts, but the distance is not as great as it appears. In Acts we find Paul evangelizing among rulers and using the highest ideals of conduct and the central concerns of religion to lead them to Christianity: when Felix and Drusilla asked Paul to talk about this religion, "he discoursed about righteousness and self-control and the future judgement" (24.24f). No Roman official is yet told that the Christians' God is the one from whom they derive their authority (cf. John 19.11), but it is made clear in the story of the shipwreck that the Roman escort owed their lives to the God who is bringing Paul to Jerusalem. "Have no fear, Paul. It is necessary for you to stand before Caesar, and, behold, God has given you the lives of all who

sail with you" (27.24). If Acts is a plea for the recognition of
Christianity, Luke in return offers to the State the protection
of the true and living God.

Gärtner's exhaustive study of the Areopagus speech has
established Luke's debt to the missionary methods of Hellenistic Judaism.[1] Gärtner's anxiety to show the Jewish and O.T.
affinities of the speech has led him, however, to underrate the
essential ambiguity of the apologetics. The object is to convert
the hearers to faith in the one living God of the O.T., but the
method is to appeal to accepted philosophical notions so that the
Greeks may be led by their own philosophy to true worship.
The closest example of the method used in Acts 14 and 17 is
to be found in the Wisdom of Solomon 13—15; in both cases
the absurdity of worshipping idols (or gods who are like man) is
shown up by contrasting these creaturely things with God the
Creator of all, and it is assumed that everyone should be able
to recognize the absurdity. There is, as Gärtner rightly main-
tains, no essential difference between the passages in Acts and
the Wisdom of Solomon and Romans 1.[2] Our purpose here is
not to discuss whether the Areopagus speech is Pauline, but
to reaffirm that it owes its form and content to Diaspora propaganda. This is one more debt of Luke to the missionary tradition of Hellenistic Judaism. Whether or not Paul spoke like
this in Lystra and Athens, Luke himself was addressing his
non-Christian readers through these two speeches, using the

[1] Bertil Gärtner, *The Areopagus Speech and Natural Revelation*, Acta Semin-
arii Neotestamentici Upsaliensis XXI (Uppsala, 1955); e.g., 252, on the
similarities between Sap. Sal. 13-15, Rom. 1, Acts 17: "This tradition can,
in all essentials, be classified as Jewish Diaspora propaganda."

[2] H. P. Owen, "The Scope of Natural Revelation in Rom. I and Acts
XVII", *N.T.S.*, v (1958-9), 133-43, tries to distinguish between Sap. Sal.
13 on the one hand and Rom. 1 and Acts 17 on the other. His main point,
that neither Rom. nor Acts assumes that God can be known as Creator of
the world through the exercise of natural reason, is not supported by his
exegesis; the argument against idolatry in Rom. and Acts only has force
on the assumption that the Gentiles have failed to recognize what it was
possible for them to know, viz., that it was wrong to worship created things
in place of the Creator. This is also the assumption behind Sap. Sal. 13-15,
and any variations on the theme, about the extent to which natural revelation was understood, are unimportant.

well-tried arguments developed by Greek-speaking Jewish apologists. The only specifically Christian element is the mention of Christ who will come to judge in Acts 17.31; the resurrection of "the divinely appointed man" has made the judgement certain, and gives a new urgency to the old arguments.

Finally, a key theological idea in Luke-Acts derives from the vocabulary of Hellenistic Judaism. Professor G. D. Kilpatrick has pointed out that two Lucan technical words, ἔλευσις and εὐαγγελίζεσθαι, come from this environment and no other;[1] we shall try now to show that Luke's theology of repentance comes from the same Jewish background.

The words μετανοέω and μετάνοια occur very frequently in Luke-Acts in comparison with the rest of the N.T.[2] Although Luke uses these terms to apply to repentance from individual sins (Luke 17.3f; Acts 8.22) as well as to signify the change of heart that Israel is called on to undergo (Luke 3.3, following Mark 1.4; 16.30; Acts 2.38; 3.19; 5.31), his usage is dominated by the idea that repentance is the great step a Gentile takes when he leaves behind his old religious or philosophical beliefs and turns to the living God. Repentance is for Luke primarily a term of proselytism, and this makes him use it both more frequently than other N.T. writers and in a more restricted sense.

Luke adopts the term "preaching of repentance", and similar phrases, as the best way to describe the Gentile mission. Luke 24.44ff, Jesus' exposition of the scriptures to his disciples after the Resurrection, is a thoroughly Lucan passage. It emphasizes, in the Lucan manner, that everything that has happened was foretold in the scriptures, particularly that "the Messiah should suffer" (cf. Luke 24.26; Acts 3.18; 17.3). The conclusion states that "it is written . . . that repentance for the forgiveness of sins is to be preached in the Messiah's name to all the Gentiles

---

[1] "Acts VII.52 ΕΛΕΥΣΙΣ", *J.T.S.*, xlvi (1945), 136–45; the comment on εὐαγγελίζεσθαι is to be found in an article, "Scribes, Lawyers, and Lucan Origins", *J.T.S.*, N.S., i (1950), 58.

[2] See Behm, Wurthwein in Kittel, *Th.Wb.z.N.T.*, iv (Stuttgart, 1942), 972–1004.

—beginning from Jerusalem". Luke has applied the summary of John the Baptist's preaching (Luke 3.3; Mark 1.4) to the Gentile mission. After Peter told the Jerusalem Church about the first and crucial Gentile conversion, the conversion of Cornelius, they used the word "repentance" to sum up what had happened: "Why, God has given repentance unto life to the Gentiles also" (11.18). Paul at Athens proclaimed that God was now calling "all men everywhere to repent", and the context makes it plain that the term is drawn from the vocabulary of Jewish proselytism rather than from a specifically Christian idea of repentance. God has not overlooked times of ignorance of the Christian gospel—there was nothing to overlook, because Jesus had not yet come—but he has overlooked the Gentile ignorance of him as Creator, which it had always been possible for them to know.[1] The new fact, that Christ is to come as judge, merely adds urgency to an old challenge.

This leads us to see the limitation on the meaning of the term which Luke must maintain because of its Jewish origin. As repentance is something that could be achieved under the old dispensation, in Christian times it can only be the first step on the way from unbelief to belief. Luke is forced to change the words about the mission of the Twelve in Mark 6.12, καὶ ἐξελθόντες ἐκήρυξαν ἵνα μετανοῶσιν, to ἐξερχόμενοι δὲ διήρχοντο κατὰ τὰς κώμας εὐαγγελιζόμενοι (9.6). Repentance for Luke is something preliminary, and he is here bound to substitute for it the word for the comprehensive proclamation of the gospel.[2] Similarly, in the words of Jesus which we have already mentioned (Luke 24.47), the proclamation of repentance to the Gentiles was qualified by the phrase "in the Messiah's name", and the Jerusalem Church to which Peter reported Cornelius's conversion called it repentance "unto life" (εἰς ζωήν).

Luke believed that the preliminary proclamation of repentance was of importance in the Gentile mission. When Paul, in

[1] But see H. P. Owen, op. cit.
[2] Conzelmann, *Die Mitte der Zeit* (Tübingen, 1954), 84, Eng. tr., 99.

his efforts to convert King Agrippa, described the preaching he undertook in obedience to the heavenly vision he said that he urged Jews and Gentiles "to repent and turn to God, performing works worthy of repentance" (26.20). Only the vision is specifically Christian; the vocabulary he adopts to explain what he did as a result of the vision is deliberately couched in terms of general religious significance so that Agrippa would understand, and perhaps accept for himself, the conversion he is preaching. Conversion to the living God and the good works that follow conversion are the important first steps, and the Christian content of conversion can be added to this in good time. The two stages were carefully distinguished by Paul in his farewell speech to the Ephesian elders when he said that he had witnessed "to Jews and the Greeks repentance towards God, and faith in our Lord Jesus Christ" (20.21; cf. 19.4 and Heb. 6.1–4). If the Jews now need to repent, that is because they have forgotten Moses and the prophets and put themselves in the position of the Gentiles, as poor Dives realized too late (Luke 16.30f).

In most, but not all, cases, Luke's use of the term seems to be drawn from the language of proselytism developed in Hellenistic Judaism. The Rabbis also developed a technical term for repentance which had no precise O.T. equivalent (תְּשׁוּבָה), but they never seem to have used it to designate the step a Gentile took when he became a proselyte. One of the few passages about repentance in which the Gentiles are mentioned is Pesikt. R. 156 a/b: "Gentiles who have not become proselytes are excluded from repentance";[1] repentance and becoming a proselyte are completely different things. Repentance is the resumption of a right attitude to God, which Israel is called on to make before the Messiah can come.[2] It is not the first step from heathen belief to be taken by Gentile proselytes.[3]

In Hellenistic Judaism, on the other hand, μετανοέω and

---

[1] Quoted by Wurthwein in Kittel, *Th.Wb.z.N.T.*, iv.992.

[2] The doctrine of one school of Rabbis is admirably summed up by Peter in Acts 3.19ff.

[3] See Wurthwein, op. cit., 991ff; Billerbeck, i.162–72.

μετάνοια came to be used to serve the Gentile mission in the period following the making of the LXX translation.[1]

In the three cases of the use of μετάνοια in the Wisdom of Solomon it refers to God's offer of repentance to Gentiles as well as to Jews.

> Thou hast mercy on all, because thou art able
>     to do all,
> And thou overlookest men's sins that they may
>     repent.
> For thou lovest all that is,
> And abhorrest nothing thou hast made;
> Thou wouldest never have fashioned anything
>     thou hatest.
>
> (11.23f; cf. 12.10,19)

The Sibylline Oracles, while much more nationalist in tone, still remain true to their missionary purpose in offering repentance to the Gentiles. In the Fourth Book the phrase δοῦναι μετάνοιαν occurs, which is used twice in Acts. (Cf. 2 Tim. 2.25, and in the Apostolic Fathers.)[2] "O ill-starred mortals, let not these things be, and drive not the Great God to divers deeds of wrath; but have done with swords and moanings and killings of men, and deeds of violence, and wash your bodies whole in ever-running rivers, and, stretching your hands to heaven, seek forgiveness for your former deeds, and with praises ask pardon (ἱλάσκεσθε) for your bitter ungodliness. God will grant repentance (θεὸς δώσει μετάνοιαν) and will not slay: He will stay his wrath once more if with one accord ye practise godliness in your heart" (lines 163–70).[3] This is an appeal to

[1] The word μετάνοια is not used in the full religious sense of "repentance" in the LXX translation of the Hebrew scriptures. The verb μετανοέω is sometimes used to translate נחם.

[2] See Conzelmann in Dibelius, *Die Pastoralbriefe, Hdb.z.N.T.* (3rd edition, Tübingen, 1955), 85f. Conzelmann's assertion, *Die Mitte der Zeit* (Tübingen 1954), 85 (Eng. tr., 100), that this expression in Acts is merely a stock phrase which has lost its original meaning, is unwarranted.

[3] Text ed. Geffcken (Leipzig, 1902); tr. H. C. O. Lanchester in Charles *Apocrypha and Pseudepigrapha* (Oxford, 1913), ii.396.

men to become proselytes, to renounce violence, to be baptized and to pray. In this way all men can receive the reward of God's gift of repentance.

Besides these scattered occurrences of μετάνοια, which illustrate its special use in appealing to Gentiles to become Jews, there are two long passages in the missionary literature of Hellenistic Judaism devoted to its praise.

The first occurs in the *Prayer of Asenath*, which tells how Asenath, the daughter of Pentephres the Priest, turned from the Egyptian gods and became a Jewish proselyte in order that she might marry Joseph. She smashed up her idols and began to fast after Joseph had refused to kiss her because her mouth was polluted with food offered to idols. "And she broke into a great sweat as she heard these words from Joseph, and as he spoke to her in the name of the Most High God. Then she wept with long and bitter weeping and repented from her gods which she worshipped and the idols to which she prayed . . ."(ix). After seven days fasting she prayed a long prayer of repentance, remembering that the God of the Hebrews was true and living and merciful, and that he did not take account of the sin of the humble, particularly when they had sinned in ignorance (xi). At the end of her prayer the Archangel Michael appeared to her and told her that God had heard her prayer and that her name was written in the Book of Life. Her name will be no longer "Asenath" but "City of Refuge", "because many nations will flee to you, and will settle under your wings, and through you will many nations be sheltered, and those who come to the Most High God through repentance will be guarded under your walls" (xv). Asenath is portrayed as the guardian and type of all proselytes, and is admitted to Israel by eating the bread of life and drinking the cup of immortality and being anointed with the ointment of incorruption.

Immediately after Michael has announced Asenath's new name we find this hymn to Repentance. "Repentance is the daughter of the Most High, and she earnestly entreats the Most High God on behalf of all who repent, for He is the Father of repentance, and she is the crown and guardian of all virgins, loving you exceedingly and making requests for you every hour from the Most High; and he will grant to all who repent a place of rest in the heavens and will restore everyone who repents"[1] (xv). It is clear from the context that repentance is the great response to the mercy of God which proselytes make, and that the writer of the story is praising repentance and showing the honour in which God holds those who repent in order to win new converts.

The concluding two sections of Philo's *Concerning the Virtues*, on Repentance and on Nobility, are designed to show the Gentile reader the way to enter "the best of commonwealths" (175) and to assure him that his status in Israel will be equal to that of the best of the Jews, for the law values each man for his own sake and disregards his ancestry in awarding praise and blame (227).[2] Again Repentance is painted in glowing colours; it means passing from darkness to light. Those who turn their back on vanity and the mythical fables on which they have been brought up, and honour God the Creator in place of those who were no gods, are joyfully welcomed into the family of the Jewish people. "So therefore all those who did not at the first acknowledge their duty to reverence the Founder and Father of all, yet afterwards embraced the creed of one instead of a multiplicity of sovereigns, must be held to be our dearest friends and closest kinsmen. They have shown the godliness of heart which above all leads to friendship and affinity, and we must rejoice with them. As if, though blind at the first they had recovered their sight and had come from the deepest darkness to behold the most radiant light" (179).[3] Repentance is like a decisive change from sickness to health (176; cf. *Abr.* 26); it is the way the proselyte must follow.

It seems clear that μετάνοια is a term used in Hellenistic Judaism in its mission to the Gentiles and that "repentance" does not have this strong and particular association in Rabbinic Judaism. In the N.T. repentance is used like this by later

---

[1] Cf. Heb. 6.6; Barn. 6.11.
[2] Cf. Rom. 2.5–12, etc.
[3] Tr. F. H. Colson, Leob Classical Library, Philo, viii (London, 1939), 273.

writers, especially by Luke, who seems to be employing the term to show his non-Christian readers the way into Christianity and to show his Christian readers how to begin to evangelize their neighbours. We conclude that this is a further debt he owes to Hellenistic Judaism.

With a short note we may close. In Acts 24.25 there is a curious summary of the topics covered by Paul when he was asked to tell Felix and Drusilla about faith in the Messiah: διαλεγομένου δὲ αὐτοῦ περὶ δικαιοσύνης καὶ ἐγκρατείας καὶ τοῦ κρίματος τοῦ μέλλοντος. . . . This type of apologetic, where moral virtues are pressed on the hearers with urgency because the judgement is coming, is naturally found in Hellenistic Jewish missionary literature. The passages already quoted from the Wisdom of Solomon (6.1–9) and the Sibylline Oracles (iv.163–78) are good examples. "God will grant repentance and will not slay: he will stay his wrath once more if with one accord ye practise precious godliness (εὐσεβίην περίτιμον) in your hearts" (Sib. Or. iv.168–70). The two virtues mentioned in Acts, however, are not the obvious ones to choose, either for themselves or in combination.[1] For that reason it is significant that they occur together in two apologetic books of Diaspora Judaism. In the Epistle of Aristeas 277 Pharaoh asked why the majority of men never became virtuous. The answer he was given by one of the Jewish translators ended, "The habit of virtue is a hindrance to those who are devoted to a life of pleasure because it enjoins upon them the preference of *temperance* and *righteousness*. For it is God who is the master of these things (ἐγκράτειαν δὲ κελεύει καὶ δικαιοσύνην προτιμᾶν. ὁ δὲ θεὸς πάντων ἡγεῖται τούτων)" (278).[2] Self-control and righteousness are brought forward in an apologetic situation as the two virtues enjoined by God. The same combination is found in Philo. In his discourse on Repentance he says that a man must not only turn to revere the Creator

---

[1] ἐγκράτεια is not precise enough to provide a reference to Felix's sexual irregularities; *Beginnings*, iv.305.

[2] Text ed. P. Wendland (Leipzig, 1900); tr. H. T. Andrews in Charles, op. cit., ii (Oxford, 1913), 118.

before his creatures but should also change to virtue from "that malignant mistress, vice". "This means passing from ignorance to knowledge of things which it is disgraceful not to know, from senselessness to good sense, from incontinence to *continence*, from injustice to *justice*, from timidity to boldness (ἐξ ἀκρατείας εἰς ἐγκράτειαν, ἐξ ἀδικίας εἰς δικαιοσύνην, ἐξ ἀτολμίας εἰς θαρραλεότητα) " (*De virtutibus*, 180).[1] The final transition, from timidity to confidence or boldness, is significant; it probably represents the confidence which comes to a man who knows that he is both God-loving and God-beloved (θεοφιλὴς καὶ φιλόθεος, 184). We may contrast it with the fear with which Felix heard about the judgement to come (ἔμφοβος γενόμενος), and speculate whether the two virtues of self-control and righteousness might not have been combined in Jewish missionary practice with a warning about God's judgement, to produce either fear or godly confidence in those who heard. There is not enough evidence to decide whether or not Luke has reproduced completely a common missionary formula, but we can affirm that the summary of Paul's preaching given here is typical of a certain approach to Gentiles which was made by Jews of the Dispersion.

[1] Tr. F. H. Colson, Loeb, viii (London, 1939). Cf. the list of the most necessary virtues, *De Josepho*, 153: σωφροσύνη, αἰδώς, ἐγκράτεια, and δικαιοσύνη.

———◆———

# CHAPTER SEVEN

# THE CENTRAL THEOLOGICAL
# PURPOSE OF ACTS

MANY OF the important doctrines in Acts have not been discussed, or have been treated very briefly. The question of Lucan eschatology has not been specifically raised, nor have the Lucan doctrines of the Church and the Spirit, of baptism, and of soteriology; natural theology and the relationship between gospel and law have only been mentioned in passing. Part of the reason for these omissions is that most of the topics are covered in the standard introductions and commentaries; where new ground is being broken, the discussion inevitably concentrates more on Luke's Gospel than would be allowable here, as, for example, in Conzelmann's outstanding study of Lucan theology, *Die Mitte der Zeit*.[1]

The more important reason for concentrating on a few limited questions is that in discussing these the way has been prepared for isolating Luke's peculiar theological message. By seeing him as a theologian of his time, we are also able to recognize the distinctive witness which he made to that generation.

One conclusion has emerged from the preceding chapters. We have seen that Luke's theological presuppositions are those which were shared by other theologians in the first half of the second century; he was one of the fore-runners of the so-called "catholic" period in the history of Christian thought. This is indicated by the way he regarded the Apostolic Age as normative and as part of salvation history, by his attitude to the Jews, by the way he used the O.T., and by the comprehensive collection of Christological titles which he had inherited. An eschatology which puts the End into the indefinite future, a

[1] Eng. tr., *The Theology of St Luke* (London, 1960).

pneumatology which confines the work of the Spirit to open and tangible effects, and a clear conception that heresy began when the apostles died (20.29), all point to the same conclusion. Luke took it for granted that the Churches were objective historical bodies with an established ministry and sacraments, and that salvation was ratified by entering their fellowship and submitting to their discipline. Of course, the thought of Paul was not as far removed from this objective ecclesiology as used to be supposed, but in Paul there is a dimension of hiddenness which is lacking in Luke. To Luke nothing of God's saving work in history is hidden; at Pentecost it was completely revealed to any who would listen.

This view of Lucan theology was put forward by a group of German theologians at the end of the last century who had been influenced by the Tübingen school, without accepting Baur's position that Acts was the conscious "synthesis" to the "thesis" and "antithesis" represented by the Judaizers and Paul. Their position is summed up in Jülicher's famous apophthegm, which was often quoted at the time: "Paul is not Judaized and Peter Paulinized, but both are Lucanized, that is, Catholicized."[1] Its main exponent to-day is Ernst Käsemann,[2] but there have always been critics ready to point out the way in which Luke had declined from the "Mysticism of Paul the Apostle".[3] Many scholars have continued to maintain

---

[1] *Einleitung in das N.T.* (1894; 7th ed., Tübingen, 1931), 431; tr. by McGiffert, *Beginnings*, ii.384 n 2. This was the point of view adopted by, among others, Bruno Bauer; A. Ritschl; F. Overbeck; H. J. Holtzmann, *Hand-Commentar z. N.T.*, 1.2 (Freiburg, 1899), 321; P. Wendland. *Die Urchr. Literaturformen, Hdb.z.N.T.*, 1.3 (2nd and 3rd ed., Tübingen, 1912), 320f; H. Windisch, *Beginnings*, ii.298–348.

[2] E.g., "Neutestamentliche Fragen von Heute", *Z.Th.K.*, 54 (1957), 1–21, at 20f.

[3] E.g., M. Kiddle, "The Passion Narrative in St Luke's Gospel", *J.T.S.*, xxxvi (1935), 267–80, at 279; T. E. Bleiben, "The Gospel of Luke and the Gospel of Paul", *J.T.S.*, xlv (1944), 134–40; Philipp Vielhauer, "Zum 'Paulinismus' der Apg.", *Evangelische Theologie* (1952), 1–15; C. F. Evans, "The Kerygma", *J.T.S.*, N.S., vii (1956), 25–41, at 41: "What is absent from Acts is any strong eschatological accent, the scandal of the cross and redemption thereby, and a doctrine of present union with Christ in his resurrection life."

that Luke presented the primitive theology, but they also have shown it to be a "catholic" and comprehensive theology which contained the doctrines of the rest of the N.T. in the framework of God's plan for men's salvation.[1]

In Chapter One we have suggested that the nearest parallel to Luke's catholic theology of history is to be found in the writings of Justin Martyr, and this parallel, even more than the general character of the theology, has led us to date the composition of Acts in the first half of the second century. Luke's theology shows these traces of "early catholicism" because he lived at a time when the organized Church could scarcely entertain any other theology: the pressure of the End had given way to the pressure of a continuing historical future, and the rich and varied traditions inherited from the past had to be fused, consciously or unconsciously, into a coherent body of doctrine.

But books are not usually written simply to expound a general point of view. Luke-Acts was not composed to provide us with an "early catholic" Church history, but to embody a particular message; the catholic nature of the undertaking arose from the author's unconscious presuppositions rather than from his conscious purpose, in as far as they can be distinguished. Working from the foundations laid in the previous six chapters, we must now attempt to define his central purpose. The task is not so much to suggest a purpose which has never been suggested before, but to attempt to put the existing suggestions into a proper perspective.

The conclusion to which we have been driven is that Luke-Acts was primarily an attempt to persuade educated Romans to become Christians; it was an "apology" in outward form but, like all true apologies, it had the burning inner purpose of bringing men to the faith. The use of the term "apology" does not imply that Acts was chiefly designed to gain official recognition for Christianity. That would clearly be an inadequate description of the central purpose of the book, because it

---

[1] E.g., C. H. Dodd, *The Apostolic Preaching and its Developments* (London, 1936).

would leave large portions out of account, as well as excluding most of Luke's Gospel. Attempts have been made to avoid this objection to the view that Acts was narrowly apologetic by supposing that a full statement of the nature of Christianity was a necessary part of the case to be presented to the Romans. B. S. Easton, for example, has argued that Luke was a liberal Jew who was asking for Christianity to be recognized as a *religio licita* because it was, despite its large Gentile member-ship, still part of Judaism.[1] There is truth in this contention, but it fails to do justice to the evangelical purpose of the work as a whole. The neutrality of the dedication to the two volumes in Luke 1.1–4, which explains to an educated public that Luke is about to set out an accurate account of Christianity's history from the beginning in order to correct and supplement the knowledge they had already gathered,[2] should not mislead us into thinking that he was on the defensive. As we have seen in the last chapter, studied objectivity characterized the prefaces to Hellenistic Jewish attempts to win educated converts for the faith, and Luke-Acts in this, as in other ways, belongs to the same *genre*. A work which was concerned with the irresistible progress of the Word of God from Jerusalem to Rome can hardly be said to be defensive. All the stylistic indications that Luke had shaped his history according to his intention to preach the gospel,[3] together with the nature of the dedicatory introduction, show that the primary purpose of Luke-Acts was to lead an educated reading public to embrace the Christian faith.[4]

Once this is established, the other suggestions about Luke's purpose fall into place. They can be shown to depend on the

---

[1] "The Purpose of Acts" (1936), reprinted in *Early Christianity: The Purpose of Acts and Other Papers* (London, 1955), 33–118.

[2] See H. J. Cadbury, *Beginnings*, ii.489–510.

[3] See Dibelius, *Studies* (London, 1956), 102, 136f, and *passim*. Dibelius has failed to see that Luke was primarily concerned with preaching to unbelievers; cf. 135.

[4] Not, of course, just Theophilus; the dedication does not imply that he was the chief target of the work, but that Luke intended to publish his book for the educated world to read; see Cadbury, *The Making of Luke-Acts* (N.Y., 1927; repr. London, 1958), 204, and A. D. Nock, Review of Dibelius's *Aufsätze, Gnomen*, 25 (1953), 501.

theme which he has adopted to give unity to his evangelistic treatise: the movement up to Jerusalem, and from Jerusalem to Rome.

First, he used this scheme of events to show that the fortunes of Jesus and the Church were governed at every turn by the hand of God. Everything that happened was inevitable and fore-ordained, and could be discovered, in the last resort, in the pages of the O.T.[1] It was no accident that Jesus died in Jerusalem or that the rejection of the gospel by Jerusalem led to Paul's arrival in Rome. Human decision was almost completely excluded at the crucial moments of the story, and Peter and Paul's movements were controlled by supernatural direction from the Holy Spirit and angels and visions whenever a decisive step had to be taken. To anyone who was prepared to see the signs of God's activity in the success of a religious movement, it could be seen here in the unprecedented growth of Christianity from the smallest beginnings, a growth which depended entirely on God's initiative. The success of Christianity, despite all the sets-backs it encountered, was used to support its claim to be the only true religion.

Second, as we have seen in Chapter Two, the movement from Jerusalem to Rome was not meant to be the story of the first preaching of the gospel in the main cities of the Empire. Acts is not primarily a history of Christian missions. It is the account of how the Church discovered its true nature in the way God dealt with it on the path from Jerusalem to Rome; the Church discovered its independent destiny when Paul reached Rome and finally turned from the Jews to the Gentiles. The educated Roman reader was being told, first and foremost, that the Church had been designed for him by God, rather than that the gospel had been brought to him by Paul. Although Jerusalem remained the city where his salvation had been achieved in the death and resurrection of Jesus Christ, Rome had been chosen as the city where the Church discovered its true rôle in the world. The Church was not simply a genuine form of the old Jewish religion which the Roman authorities had recog-

---

[1] Cadbury, op. cit., 303–6; Dibelius, op. cit., *passim*.

nized and even protected; it was the only true Israel. It alone could understand the riddles in the Bible, the book which was the distinguishing mark of Judaism, and it alone should be recognized as the true organized representative of Jewish monotheism. But Acts was not only designed to show that Christianity had a far greater claim to recognition than Judaism; it demonstrated by the examples of Cornelius and Sergius Paulus (and Publius, Acts 28.7ff) that some well-placed Romans had already adopted it as their faith in the earliest days. The divinely ordained movement from Jerusalem to Rome corresponded to the current of missionary success; what the Jews had rejected was now an open possibility for the Romans. The fact that educated Romans could believe and had believed was a strong argument for others to follow their example. Luke-Acts not only showed that God had prepared the Church for them by his intervention in history, but it also taught the salient points of the faith which it was asking them to accept. The speeches in Acts fulfil many functions, but not the least important is that of repeating over and over again the framework of the Christian faith as understood by Luke and his Church.[1]

We have seen that Luke's history of the Church demonstrated the power of the true and living God, and that it opened up to educated citizens of the Empire the possibility of belief. It also demonstrated the innocence of the Christians of any revolutionary political tendencies, and this is the third point.[2] The political accusations made against Jesus and the Christian leaders were completely groundless, as the decisions of Pilate and Herod and the rest showed. The accusations arose either from fear in certain quarters that the adoption of Christianity would involve financial loss, or from the hostility of the Jews.

---

[1] Dibelius, "The Speeches in Acts and Ancient Historiography", op. cit., 138–85. See now the work of Ulrich Wilckens cited above, 119 n 1.

[2] The classic statement of the argument is by Joh. Weiss, *Ueber die Absicht und den litterarischen Charakter der Apg.* (Göttingen, 1897); see also Overbeck, Introduction to de Wette's commentary (Eng. tr., London, 1875), 23ff, and B. S. Easton, op. cit. Weiss argues that the twin political and religious question of the recognition of Christianity was the chief concern of Acts, 54–60.

The Jews often linked the political charge with a religious one, that Christians were teaching the violation of the Law of Moses; Roman officials always judged Christians innocent of the first and, if they held themselves incompetent to decide the second, the accused Christians always made it clear that it, too, had no substance. The Church came to maturity in Rome by way of Paul's suffering as a Roman prisoner, just as Jesus had come to reign in Jerusalem by way of death on a Roman cross, but in both cases it was innocent suffering, and the central position given to Jerusalem, with the emphasis on the ful-fillings of O.T. prophecies there, showed that this innocent religion was also the true Judaism. Johannes Weiss has rightly emphasized the connection between the establishment of the Church's political innocence and the establishment of its undeviating adherence to the true beliefs of Judaism, but it is drawing too narrow a conclusion to infer that Luke's argument was simply that "the State should confer on the new religion the protection granted to the old".[1] Luke may have incidentally desired legal recognition, but his primary aim was some-thing greater; a legal case could have been better presented in a shorter and more direct form. The repeated and dramatic demonstration that Christianity was both politically innocent and religiously the true fulfilment of the expectations of Juda-ism was not a legal but an evangelistic argument. Luke wanted to persuade Romans that, as Christianity was not a subversive

---

[1] Op. cit., 59. Conzelmann in a review of the third edition of Haenchen's Commentary, *Theologische Literaturzeitung*, 85 (1960), 241–50 at 244f, points out that there was no such thing as the legal concept of a *religio licita*; it was constructed on one occasion, *ad hoc*, by Tertullian (*Apol.* 21.1?). This additional evidence confirms an earlier observation, *Die Mitte der Zeit* (Tübingen, 1954), 117–24, Eng. tr. (London, 1960), 138–44, that Christians in Acts never sought acquittal in a Roman court by appealing to any religious toleration which may have been extended to Jews; the relation between Christianity and Judaism was, from a legal point of view, irrele-vant (Acts 18.14ff). Conzelmann goes on to argue, however, that Luke was employing a double argument, emphasizing the Church's continuity with Israel (for ecclesiastical consumption) and the gulf between the Church and "the Jews" (for imperial consumption). This distinction of audience seems artificial; both ideas were, in the end, important for both audiences.

movement and was the consummation of an ancient and honourable monotheism, it was eminently worthy of their allegiance. In doing so, he has put the leaders of unrepentant Judaism in a bad light by showing how they used the mob to stir up trouble against innocent men. If Acts was written between A.D. 115 and 130, it was written between the Jewish rising in the East in 116 and the Bar Cochba rebellion in 132; in those circumstances Luke's dissociation of Christianity from disaffected Judaism would have been a prudent step, and a necessary one if Romans were to be converted. He showed that the earthly Jerusalem, representing Jewish aspirations for political independence, was to remain in subjection, while the salvation worked out in the heavenly city, despite the malevolence of the earthly, had been handed over to the Gentiles in Rome (cf. Luke 21.24). The account of the movement from Jerusalem to Rome is again made to express in symbolic form an important part of Luke's apologetic theology.

It is important to see that Luke's primary aim was to preach the gospel to unbelievers. Although a theological message for the Church inevitably flowed from this venture in apologetics, that was strictly a subsidiary concern. This should not surprise Christians in the twentieth century, for the most far-reaching contemporary examination of the Church's theology has come from a man who began by finding that he did not know how to preach to an unbelieving world. Karl Barth has in fact defined the discipline of dogmatic theology by subordinating it to the Church's preaching mission: dogmatic theology is the Church's continual attempt to criticize its own proclamation of the gospel by the standards God has given it. The important theological positions to which Luke called the attention of his Church in Luke-Acts followed directly from his central purpose. In drawing the attention of educated Romans to the magnitude of what God had done in Jesus' death and resurrection, he was at the same time reminding the Church of the power to which it owed its existence, and warning it not to betray its trust.

A number of specific warnings to the Church flow from

Luke's apologetic and evangelistic arguments. First, he warned Christians not to pin their hopes on a literal and immediate fulfilment of the apocalyptic expectations inherited from Judaism. Not only might such beliefs lure them into joining in Jewish insurrections, but they would frustrate God's purpose for them by turning their attention away from the ordinary world of men. Romans holding influential positions would not be impressed by such religious enthusiasm. So we read that, when the disciples asked Jesus just before his ascension whether he would then restore the kingdom to Israel, he firmly prohibited all such speculation and told them to prepare themselves instead to receive the power which would drive them out from Jerusalem to Rome as his witnesses (Acts 1.6–8). This was Jesus' last and, in some ways, his most important command. Luke believed that Jesus' intention was to establish the Church as a power in the Gentile world, and his own attempt in Luke-Acts to further this destiny inevitably meant reminding the Church of where its responsibilities lay: not in nourishing apocalyptic hopes centred on Jerusalem, but in witnessing to the Gentiles.

Second, part of the gospel which Luke proclaimed to Gentiles was that God had established his Church as an independent entity for them. Paul fully discovered this only when he was forced to turn from the Jews to the Gentiles in Rome, but this discovery lends added weight to his last testimony to the leaders of the Church, the speech addressed to the Ephesian elders in Miletus (Acts 20.17–38).[1] When Paul came to Rome to die for the faith, he set the seal on the Church's recognition that it had superseded Judaism, and the Testament of Paul to the Church leaders was designed to fit the Church to perform this newly realized function. The local churches were the congregations into which the Gentiles were to be welcomed, and for that reason Paul warned the appointed leaders, the elders or bishops, to

---

[1] Johannes Munck, "Discours d'adieu dans le N.T. et dans la littérature biblique", *Goguel Festschrift* (Neuchatel and Paris, 1950), 155–70, esp. 159–61, 164, 169: "The death of the Apostles marks the advent of the Antichrist."

be on their guard against the internal disruptive forces of heresy (20.28-30). Similarly, in Chapter Four we saw that Luke has assumed that the early Church had arrived at an orderly arrangement for settling the potentially disruptive relations between Jewish and Gentile Christians. This was a problem which faced his own Church, to which he believed the apostolic age offered the solution. We also suggested that the Jerusalem Decree, besides codifying the terms of this agreement, was probably meant to provide a test for use against antinomian heresy. Acts shows the Church discovering itself as the only true heir to the universal promises in the O.T., but in discovering that it was a people separate from Judaism, it also had to discover ways of guarding the purity of its faith and the integrity of its organization. Luke's insistence on this point sprang from his desire to win the allegiance of Romans to the only religion foretold and established by God, and his apologetic arguments necessarily involved him in showing to the Church the means by which it should preserve the unity achieved in the apostolic age. Luke's own attempts to forward the Church's mission involved his preaching the Church's unity.

Finally, by finishing his work when Paul arrived at Rome, Luke has tried to show the Church where its future lay. He believed Christianity was fitted by nature to be the religion of the world. This seems to be the reason why he made Paul his hero. The usual reasons which have been advanced to explain Paul's prominence do not seem to explain the evidence. Luke can hardly have belonged to a specifically Pauline party in the Church, because he made no distinction between Paul's theological position and that of the other Church leaders. He knew that there were some characteristic features in Pauline theology to do with justification and grace, but he represented such features as merely additions to the standard preaching (13.38) which, in any case, the Apostles also believed (15.10f). He took trouble to make it clear that Paul did not advocate the abandonment of the Law by Jews and, on the other hand, he insisted that there was nothing specifically Pauline in the insistence by all the Church leaders that Gentile Christians should be free from circumcision. Luke did not know Paul's epistles, and it is unlikely that he made Paul his hero because he wished to support a specifically Pauline theology, or even because he wished to explain how Gentile Christianity, deeply influenced by Christian Judaism, had been founded by Paul.[1] There is no evidence before 2 Polycarp that the Church was particularly conscious of Paul as a theologian, and the only evidence we do possess suggests that Paul was honoured for something far more practical. In Clement of Rome's epistle to the Corinthians, as we have seen in Chapter One, Paul was honoured not only for his martyrdom, but for the fact that he had reached "the western goal"—Rome—to die. It is almost certain that Peter was also martyred in Rome, but Clement did not seem to attach the same significance to the place where Peter died. He noted two things about Paul's arrival in the capital: it was the end of a preaching mission to the whole world, and it was the place where he witnessed to the rulers. The same significance is attached to Paul's last days in Rome in 2 Tim. 4.16–18.[2] The author of the Pastoral epistles has emphasized that Paul's defence before the Imperial court in Rome completed the preaching. In principle the Gentile mission was over.

Acts assumed the same view of Paul's martyrdom. As we have already seen, the book was constructed according to the pattern laid down in Jesus' last commission to his disciples: to be his witnesses in Jerusalem, and in all Judea and Samaria, and to the end of the earth. The pattern was complete, according to Luke, when Paul came to Rome to die, and whole of Acts was a plea to the Gentiles in general, and to educated Romans in particular, to accept the heritage which was prepared for them in this way. Luke has taken the traditional view of the significance of Paul's martyrdom and extended it to embrace the whole of the central period of the history of salvation. From the time when God sent Gabriel to Nazareth in Galilee to announce to Mary that she would bear Jesus who would rule over the house of Israel for ever, until the time when

[1] Overbeck, op. cit. (Eng. tr.), 22.
[2] See the discussion, 6–9 above.

Paul was brought to Rome to witness to what had happened in Jerusalem, salvation was being prepared for the Gentiles; every decision made and every journey undertaken served this one end. In Rome the witness to the rulers was made and, in principle, the Gospel was preached to all the Gentiles.

Acts affords no indication that Paul was singled out to serve a party interest. Although the author seems to be indebted to the traditional view of the significance of Paul's mission and martyrdom preserved in 1 Clement and the Pastoral epistles, he obviously believed that this was also the significance of the work of Christ and the Apostles. He was careful to show that Paul was only carrying on what Peter had begun and, by omitting an actual account of Paul's martyrdom, to emphasize that the establishment of the Church in Rome was the fruit of Christ's death and resurrection in Jerusalem. His aim was to convert his readers to Christianity, not to defend one party in the Church; the corresponding message to the Church was that its future lay in the very centre of the political world. Luke was looking forward to the time when Christianity would become the religion of the Empire, and he wanted the Church to prepare itself for the rôle.

We have come by devious routes to see the unique place which Acts occupies in the N.T. The evidence which has emerged from the previous chapters has led us to one conclusion: Luke's background, his theology, and his understanding of the Church's situation made him, in the fullest sense of the word, an apologist. The book of Acts, together with Luke's Gospel, is probably the only work in the N.T. which was specifically addressed to unbelievers. Luke believed that God had prepared the Church to receive the educated and the politically powerful as well as the poor and the outcast, and he wrote Luke-Acts to persuade men at the centre of power to abandon their lives to the service of the kingdom of God.

# INDEXES

## 1. OLD TESTAMENT

## 2. JEWISH WRITINGS

## 3. NEW TESTAMENT
*Roman numerals refer to the Tables, 43–53*

## 4. EARLY CHRISTIAN WRITERS AND WRITINGS

Roman numerals refer to the Tables, 43–53

## 5. MODERN WRITERS